D0429089

True
Believers
~~Don't~~
Ask Why

True Believers ~~Don't~~ Ask Why

JOHN FISCHER

BETHANY HOUSE PUBLISHERS
MINNEAPOLIS, MINNESOTA 55438
A Division of Bethany Fellowship, Inc.

Published by Bethany House Publishers
A Division of Bethany Fellowship, Inc.
6820 Auto Club Road, Minneapolis, Minnesota 55438

Printed in the United States of America

Library of Congress Cataloging-in-Publication Data

Fischer, John.
    True believers don't ask why / John Fischer.
       p. cm.

    1. Faith. 2. Christian life—1960– I. Title.
BT771.2.F58   1989
230—dc20   89–32730
ISBN 1-55661-055-6   CIP

To my Mother and Father
. . . still asking, seeking, knocking . . .

CONTENTS

"Why do you weep when you pray?" he asked me, as though he had known me a long time.

"I don't know why," I answered, greatly disturbed.

The question had never entered by head. I wept because—because of something inside me that felt the need for tears. That was all I knew.

"Why do you pray?" he asked me after a moment.

Why did I pray? A strange question. Why did I live? Why did I breathe?

"I don't know why," I said, even more disturbed and ill at ease. "I don't know why."

After that day I saw him often. He explained to me with great insistence that every question possessed a power that did not lie in the answer.

—Elie Wiesel from *Night*[1]

[1]Elie Wiesel, *Night* (New York: Avon, 1981). Used by permission.

ASK . . . SEEK . . . KNOCK

INTRODUCTION

*D*o you want to get well?"—surely one of the most important questions Jesus ever asked anyone. The answer is not as obvious as it may seem. Even the man to whom it was addressed didn't give a direct answer. An invalid for thirty-eight years, he responded by muttering something about never being able to get into the healing waters of the pool of Bethesda: "While I'm trying to get in, someone else goes down ahead of me." Why not a simple "Yes"? Why not an enthusiastic and glorious "Yes!"?

No doubt he didn't realize the Lord of the Universe was speaking to him. But even that knowledge might not have guaranteed a different response. Thirty-eight years is a long time to settle into the comforts of being an invalid—of always having an excuse. Being well holds more responsibilities. Jesus wanted to know what the man wanted.

He wants to know the same from us. Jesus can do little for us if we are comfortable with our place, if we have made compromising alliances with our losses and excuses for our inability to change. Too often we languish in our condition when all

11

along, Jesus stands there asking, "What do you want?" And if we don't languish, then we lull; we settle for less.

Though physical healing may be involved, it is not the main point. Jesus' question refers to life itself. *What do you want from life? What do you want from me?* "Ask and it will be given to you; seek and you will find; knock and the door will be opened to you." Then He repeats "For everyone who asks receives; he who seeks finds; and to him who knocks, the door will be opened."

The first statement is a formula—a cause and effect proposition—do this, and this will result. The second has a different emphasis—on the *person,* not the *formula.* "For everyone who asks . . . he who seeks . . . to him who knocks. . . ." Jesus is talking about a type of person. God's economy rewards the askers, the seekers, the knockers.

In the end, the process is quite simple: I ask because I don't know the answer; I seek because there's more to find; I knock because this door goes someplace.

True Believers ~~Don't~~ *Ask Why* is a chronicle of my own questionings, searchings, and poundings on the doors of my life; I have found them all rewarded in some way. If this book raises more questions than it resolves, then I will consider it a success, for its purpose is to awaken the asking, seeking, knocking heart.

But there is still one more reason for all this asking, seeking, and knocking—perhaps the most important. It is found in the teaching of Jesus on prayer.

"And when you pray, do not keep on babbling like the pagans, for they think they will be heard because of their many words. Do not be like them, for your Father knows what you need before you ask him" (Matt. 6:7–8).

So why bother? Because even though He knows what I need, He doesn't address it until I ask. It's as if the asking and the receiving are only secondary as far as the Father is concerned. He already knows what I need before I ask Him. He simply wants to hear from me, to talk with me. It's a *relationship* he desires more than anything. All this asking, seeking, and knocking is just an excuse for a nearness God longs for more than we can ever know or fathom. *God wants to be friends with us! It is for such a relationship that we were created.*

TRUE BELIEVERS DON'T ASK WHY

─────── 1 ───────

*C*hristians don't ask why because Christians already know why.

Christians have all the answers.

Christians know the reasons for things because they know the truth.

Jesus is the answer; therefore nothing can be unanswered.

If Christians ask why, it's a sign of doubt; and Christians never doubt, so true believers don't ask why.

Oh, really?

In the meantime, a Christian culture uses publishing, music, TV, and video to pour forth a continual stream of answers to every possible question this modern age can come up with—and some we haven't thought of yet. Christian bookstores are a catalogue of "how-to" books.

We are all one key, two steps, three points, or four laws away from a victorious Christian life; and this seminar, booklet, conference, film series, or talk show will provide the missing link.

"So many believers; there's so much to believe."

Our society is obsessed with answers. Psychiatry, chiropractic, holistic medicine, health food, physical fitness, brain power, vitamins, acupuncture—each of these answers rolls into town like some new Dr. Quack's Traveling Side Show, offering an elixir promising to be the cure-all for all our ills.

"Too many answers, too many connoisseurs.
Too many cancers and too many cures."

In this regard, Christians are no different from the world. Everyone wants a quick fix, and there are plenty of claims to go around. We say Jesus is the answer, but we embrace all the faddish answers of our society at the same time. Switch from a Christian talk show to a secular talk show and back again, remove the Christian lingo, and the messages are the same, although the secular solutions are a few steps ahead. By the time Christians pick them up, the issues are usually fading in the world.

The real culprit is not the false teachers and fast fix-its. Just as surely as there were the Dr. Quacks of yesterday, there will always be the instant, easy answers of today. The problem is us. We are simply not willing to live with questions.

Questions leave us vulnerable, weak, needy. They open up gaping holes in our personality, our theology, or our lifestyle. Questions force an honesty that we are unwilling to confront— an honesty that requires us to live with our lives unresolved. We don't like that, especially when we're trying to sell a theology that Christianity is the answer to every problem we face.

This morning I counted 288 question marks in the book of Job. Many were from the mouth of Job; others were spoken by his counselors who turned out to be much like the side-show con artists of today. "Who is this that obscures my counsel without knowledge?" God said of them. But surprisingly, when God finally speaks in the closing chapters, His answer to Job comes in the form of more questions—78 of them, to be exact. Of the 288 question marks in the book of Job, 78 of them belong to God; they are His answer to Job.

Sometimes God answers us with questions—questions that leave us humbled, awed, speechless, weak, and believing— believing not because we've found the answer, but because we've seen God. It doesn't matter that we have more questions now than when we started. It matters that we see God, for in the seeing, we discover that the truest answer to all our questions is to worship Him.

Don't ask me for the answers
I've only found one:
That a man leaves his darkness
When he follows the Son. [1]

—Larry Norman

[1]Written by Larry Norman. Published by J.C. Love Publishing Co. (BMI). Used by permission.

16

PART I

ASK SEEK KNOCK

$\mathcal{H}$ow many minutes have I driven up and down nameless streets unable to find the place I'm looking for—simply because I was too proud to ask? How many questions have gone unexamined because I didn't want anyone to think I didn't know the answer? How many times have people smiled and tolerated what I did for them when in fact I never asked what they wanted? How much have I done "for God" without ever asking Him what He wanted? How much emptiness have I endured because I never asked God to fill me? How much worry has eaten out my insides because I didn't want to ask for help?

The first maxim is the hardest. Asking is one of the hardest things we will ever do because it assumes a position of need.

That's why most of us pass by this statement of Jesus and never truly relate to it. We look at it like some kind of Santa Claus promise: We sit on Jesus' lap and ask for things (all of which we could do without) in a department-store culture full of nonessentials. There's nothing deprecating about that kind of asking; because we fail to take the command to ask seriously, He never takes us seriously.

Because we can't see this as more than a spiritual wish list, we dismiss the notion entirely. We don't ask because we don't seek to find out what Jesus desires in our asking.

Asking has nothing to do with sitting on Jesus' lap. Asking is a way of life lived with an open hand. To ask is to depend on someone other than yourself. It is very humbling. Asking indicates:

I don't know.
I failed.
I ran out.
I can't find it.
I'm not sure.
I don't understand.
I forgot.
I didn't listen.
I didn't care.
I was wrong.
I'm not prepared.
I need more information.
I came up short.

There's an interesting dilemma here for Christians. If Christianity is no more than a system that answers all of life's questions, then to admit any of the above shortcomings is to be something less than a good Christian. But in our own attempts to be good Christians, we undermine our need for God. We want Christianity to work. We want it to exist in a closed system where every question has an answer, every problem has a solution. We want to show the world a neat, clean, open-and-shut case for Christianity. But in the process, we unknowingly shut out God.

Claiming to be wise, we become fools; we exchange the truth of God for a lie and worship the created things (our systems, principles, and formulas) rather than the Creator—who is forever blessed. Amen (Rom. 1:25).

That's why Jesus says we should ask. Asking puts us back on track with God. It assumes a need relationship with Him—a hand-to-mouth spiritual existence. A vulnerable daily dependence. In a society that rushes to fill every felt need, that steals away the soul of a person and offers to sell it back at a price, we need to rekindle what it means to ask God.

> O God, you are my God,
> earnestly will I seek you;
> my soul thirsts for you,
> my body longs for you,
> in a dry and weary land
> where there is no water.
> —Psalm 63:1

We hear this cry of David, but we know little of this thirst because there is so much around us to drink. We live in a *wet* and weary land where there is water everywhere and not a drop to drink for our souls. We pour so much liquid on our thirst-buds that our everlasting thirst is drowned out by the temporal. And they sell this bottled water even at Christian counters.

Ask, Jesus says. Ask. It's so simple—like a child. Ask. And when you receive, keep on asking. Don't accept a fake fill. Live in your thirst and you will live in Him. Open your hand. Ask.

ASKING WHY

2

$\mathscr{T}$he bleachers in the gymnasium had been pulled out to accommodate a hundred or so students, all members of a high school Christian leadership conference. The speaker was a professional big league ball player with a string of all-star appearances. He talked of his experiences playing ball and gave his testimony about how his faith in Christ had brought meaning into his life and onto the playing field.

He spoke more than once of the beautiful wife and two children God had given him. He was indeed blessed. A big league contract, a beautiful wife and family, and a testimony. I found myself liking this kind, gentle, sincere man.

I studied the faces in the bleachers. The kids were quiet, attentive. They laughed in all the right places and turned serious when they were supposed to.

But as we filed out of the gymnasium, I noticed a feeling not unlike leaving a movie theater after a touching, warmhearted picture. You try to hold on to the fantasy, but reality slides back up against you as the good feelings evaporate into the night. If the movie was a good one and convinced you of its escape, reality may seem even harsher in that moment.

I began to think about the kids in the stands. Statistically, 50 out of 100 of these kids had parents who had decided their husbands or wives were no longer desirable, leaving them to deal with being a broken part of a home; 35 of them had been sexually abused, but no one would ever know; 65 were no longer virgins; and all of them had varying levels of anxiety about their future and the world that was waiting for them—a world that didn't guarantee any of them a job, much less a big league contract. Few would probably ever have a chance to buy a house for their own beautiful wife and family.

In the face of these statistics, the impact of the dedicated ball player and his beautiful wife and family—and yes, his testimony as well—evaporated like a movie memory in the theater parking lot.

Yet no one even seemed to notice the speaker and the students in the bleachers passing one another silently like ships in the night. The kids acted as if this were the way it was supposed to be. Famous Christian speakers give testimonies like this. Good Christian kids listen. The ballplayer had asked for questions at the end of his talk. No one had any to ask.

I believe what happened in the gymnasium that night was a microcosm of the present Christian culture in America—a Christianity full of answers to questions no one is asking.

Oh, there are questions all right, but usually they are not the real ones. The questions being asked today are all "how-to" questions: how to be successful, how to stay healthy and happy, how to maximize your resources, how to be a better Christian. And the answers crowd the shelves and displays of bookstores across the country.

But what do the answers mean? How does my faith relate to what's really happening to me? Why is everyone uncomfortable when I ask a question no one can answer? How can Christianity look so neat and orderly when life is such a mess?

True believers are not afraid to ask why.

CAMEL DU JOUR

———————— 3 ————————

PROGRAM DIRECTOR (off the air): Thanks, John, for taking some of your busy time to be on our show. Jim will talk briefly with you about your book and then open up the lines for any callers who might want to chat with you. All set?

JOHN: All set.

PROGRAM DIRECTOR: Okay. Just a few seconds now and we'll begin. (pause, then on the air) Good evening everyone! This is WCLU, Christian music for the LoHigh Valley, and it's time for HeartTalk with your host, Jim Jensen. Good evening, Jim.

JIM: And a good evening to you, Greg, and to all our listeners out there in your homes or trying to get there from work. I'm Jim Jensen with today's version of HeartTalk, and we're honored to have with us author and singer/songwriter John Fischer. John, welcome.

JOHN: Thank you, Jim.

JIM: John, your new book has an interesting title; you want to tell us about it?

JOHN: Sure, but it's kind of tough to explain this title on the radio.

JIM: I know, that's why I asked you to do it! (laughs)

JOHN: Well, the title is *Real Christians Don't Dance,* but with the *Don't* crossed out.

JIM: Now, what kind of title is that? Are you trying to tell us Christians should boogie on down to the local nightclub and dance their socks off?

JOHN: No, not really. This is not 192 pages about the subject of dancing. It's about the metaphor of dance as it relates to a believer's life in Christ. The dance is a picture of the freedom and reality of knowing Christ, and crossing the *Don't* signifies getting beyond the evangelical trappings and petty rules which crowd out that freedom.

 The book is really a "weeding-through" process of my own life growing up in an evangelical ghetto trying to determine what of my Christian experience to keep and what to throw away. This is not a "how-to" book; it's more a book of experience, of growth, of tackling some hard questions that Christians seldom address.

JIM: And what kind of response have you gotten so far?

JOHN: Well, actually, very good responses, Jim. I'm encouraged because I've been pretty honest with some of my questions and doubts about the Christian life, thinking that there must be other people out there who feel as I do and would appreciate someone willing to work out these things in public. So far, the responses seem to indicate I was right.

JIM: I hope so, John. I know my wife and I have identified a lot with your book—in fact, she took it away from me and hasn't given it back!

 Well, look at this; the lines are already lighting up. We're going to break for a commercial and we'll be back with our first caller. Don't go away!

AD #1: *Are you having a hard time making life work for you? Lost a job, your family? Does it seem ever more difficult keeping up with the successes of those around you? Well, then, the Christian Counseling Service may be for you. We have qualified, trained counselors ready to listen to your problems and to give you some practical solutions. Call us at 545–5950 for a free first consultation. Remember, at Christian Counseling Service, you'll always find someone who cares.*

JIM: Okay. Welcome back everyone; this is Jim Jensen with HeartTalk. On the line with me is John Fischer, author of *Real Christians Don't Dance* (with the *Don't* crossed out), and on the other line from South LoHigh we have Peggy. Hi, Peggy!

PEGGY: Hi, Jim.

JIM: What's on your mind today?

PEGGY: Well, Jim, you know I just love your show; I listen to it every day, but the gentleman you have on right now who says it's all right for Christians to dance, well, I just can't go along with that. It seems like just another step in the church getting more and more worldly. Pretty soon it will be all right to drink and smoke, too!

JOHN: Actually, Peggy, my whole point is to get us beyond these issues. We love to stay stuck on petty things like dancing, smoking, and drinking because then we can avoid the jealousy, hatred, prejudice, divorce, child abuse, and sexual immorality that we all know is going on in some form in our lives. It's like Jesus said about the Pharisees, "You strain at a gnat and swallow a camel." I don't think the major problem with Christians is dancing; it's camel swallowing.

JIM: John, we've got Bill on the line from Upper LoHigh. Bill, welcome to HeartTalk.

BILL: Thank you, Jim. I'm a first-time caller, though I listen to your show all the time. I'd just like to say I agree with John. I think Christians *should* dance. It's time we started having fun . . . too many long faces! (long pause)

JIM: Is that it, Bill?

BILL: Yep, that's it.

JOHN: Jim, are we speaking the same language here?

JIM: Well, we're speaking, but I'm not sure anyone's listening. At any rate, it's time for another commercial break. We'll be right back with HeartTalk after this.

AD #2: Are you having chronic health problems? Find you're getting run down, even depressed? Have you found conventional doctors, even counselors, to be inadequate for your problems? You may be suffering from improper alignment. The doctors at Kingdom Chiropractic are offering a free appointment to get you acquainted with the marvels of chiropractic care. They want to show you what a big difference a small adjustment can make in your life. Call us now at

JIM: Okay. Well, we've got time for one more caller and I have Eileen from LoHigh on the line. Eileen?

EILEEN: Hello?

JIM: Go ahead, Eileen; you're on the air.

EILEEN: I'm kind of nervous. I've never called in before; in fact, I just happened to catch your show and couldn't help noticing your guest talking about Christians being honest. You know, I'm a Christian, and for a few months now I've been working with a community action group on child abuse. Some of my Christian friends don't think I should be working with a secular organization. It's hard to say what—

JIM: Eileen, you're going to have to get to the point; we're running out of time. Is there a specific question you'd like to ask John?

EILEEN: (pause) Well . . . yes. It seems we've discovered that there's just as much child abuse in the church as there is outside of it. I even know of two pastors in this very town who are sexually abusing their children. I know because their kids have gotten in contact with our program. I don't know what to do. I try to bring this out in my own church, but I only get shut up. Even my husband doesn't want to talk about it. He says I've embarrassed him by raising this issue. Why is the church so full of hypocrites? I can't—

JIM: Eileen, I'm sorry but I'm going to have to cut you off here. We're totally out of time. Please stay on the line; I'd like to talk to you afterward. Well, John, any closing remarks?

JOHN: Wow . . . what can I say except thank you, Eileen, for telling the truth. I think this is a good example of a camel that I hope we don't swallow.

JIM: Well, that about wraps it up for today, folks. Join us again tomorrow at 5 o'clock for HeartTalk on WCLU, Christian music for the LoHigh Valley.

(music fades)

to maintain a healthy air quality for your home. What's more, they're all concerned Christians—concerned with your health and well-being. If you have chronic health problems or you simply want to make sure the air quality in your home is optimal, call us at 545–4454 for a free appointment and don't be like Sally. "She didn't know it was the air."

(Only the names have been changed . . .)

WHEN ANSWERS ARE IDOLS

4

In some cases we learn more by looking for the answer to a question and not finding it than we do from learning the answer itself.
—Dallben, from *The Book of Three* by Lloyd Alexander

*I*s the Bible a Book of Answers? Is its primary purpose to provide us with a manual for life? Do we approach the Bible as if it were a sacred vault from which specific answers can be mined—answers that will make our lives successful?

Good things can become idols. Even the actual graven images of the Old Testament were not bad in and of themselves. Some were probably admirable works of art. A thing becomes an idol when it is placed before, or in the place of, the living God. The idol can be anything—a piece of wood, the sun, the Bible, a person, or a system of answers that explains reality sufficiently for one's own experiences.

To come to God seeking anything but himself is to come with

insufficient need. A person merely seeking answers to life's questions is not asking for enough. And when someone else provides the answers to those questions, he may—intentionally or not—be doing away with another's need for God. Subtle, these things we place as other gods before Him.

We seek the security of a closed system that promises answers to life's questions long before we are interested in seeking a God who withholds them. We study the Bible as a problem-solving workbook long before we approach it as a doorway to an awesome, holy, not-to-be-pandering-to-anyone God.

Dallben was right: We learn more by *not* finding the answers, because in our deficiency we are most likely to find God. Answers can be idols. One who carries around the answers to all of life's questions in a three-ring notebook or a weekend seminar is not likely to have a vital relationship with a living God. The poor in spirit have always been more blessed than the rich.

One of my most unsettling experiences as a young Christian was to attend an introductory est meeting. Developed in 1971 by Werner Erhard, est is a highly regimented psychological training seminar through which people reprogram their own personal worlds and take responsibility for their lives. For certain people it is very successful.

Many have engineered major changes in their lives, as their honest, spirited testimonials bear out. The similarity of these testimonials to the ones I was used to hearing in church shook me up. These people were talking about how their lives had been significantly changed through the est experience, and the love and support of the group reinforced their findings. If I closed my eyes and added a "Praise the Lord" in the appropriate places, I was in church.

These people had found answers for their lives that were working at least as well as Christianity, in some cases better. My first inclination was to charge this affinity to the clever counterfeit of Satan. Only later did I realize that the real problem was a misguided Christianity that established the validity of faith on problem-solving. If Christianity is true only because it works the way we want it to, because it answers all our questions, our faith is up for grabs. Many religious and nonreligious systems answer far more questions than God ever planned on answering. When answers are idols, God is irrelevant.

Whether or not life is working for me can become an all-consuming issue. In its godlessness, est was frighteningly close to the experiences I had so far encountered in the Christian Church. In the pursuit of answers to life's questions, est and modern Christianity are dangerously similar. In the pursuit of God, they are categorically opposed. The fact that I ever found est a threat to my faith is an indication of how much importance Christianity has placed on answers versus the knowledge of the Holy One.

The problem is not how well Satan has counterfeited Christianity, but how far Christianity has digressed from its central focus in its search for the pragmatic. Making life work, being successful, answering questions, feeling good, and solving problems have become more important to the modern Christian than knowing and worshiping the true God.

Most believers know that est and Christianity don't belong in the same camp. But we all should be more concerned about how often they end up there. Actually, there are only two camps in this regard: (1) those who ask questions and love God, and (2) those who want their questions answered in a closed system that works in their own subjective experience of reality. Those in the first camp are followers of Christ; those in the second are more followers of Werner Erhard than anyone but John Denver would like to admit.

You can't have God and have your questions answered at the same time. Answers too often turn into idols. We learn more by looking for the answer to a question and not finding it than we do from finding the answer itself.

JUST A DREAM

—— 5 ——

*E*verything was in vivid color. I knew it was just a dream, but still it puzzled me. I was at a large outdoor gathering watching magicians on stage. They were doing all sorts of marvelously magical things and working their Christian testimony in edgewise. One of them, with a joker face that made me vaguely uncomfortable, tried to get me to laugh. He addressed me directly, setting me up for a punch line I was supposed to know but didn't. One of the others, who seemed to know who I was, pulled him away and went on to involve someone else in the show. I stayed a bit longer to watch, but when the magician started to levitate my two children on stage, I grabbed them and left.

There were other stages, with many events taking place simultaneously. *This dream must represent some kind of Christian festival,* I thought, *a Jesus Carnival perhaps.*

Certain faces stuck out in the crowd. One man staggered by in a dreamlike state as if he had somehow made his way from his own dream into mine. He was repeating over and over miracle phrases full of promise. He must have just heard a speaker giving a speech about the keys to life, because he carried on with these phrases as if they were hanging on an endless spiritual key chain and he was trying them one by one in the lock that hung on the door of his problems. Over and over he repeated catchphrases in a trance, oblivious to anyone and anything around him. One after another, keys turned round and round hopelessly in the lock, and he finally passed by me and faded out of my dream.

This was definitely a Christian event, but something was very wrong about it and no one was asking why. They all actually seemed to be enjoying themselves, quite unaware of the dark influences that lurked like an undertow beneath a playful surf.

Soon three teenage girls came by, with happy, clean-scrubbed faces and bouncy perms, wearing oversized sweatshirts with big letters spelling out the words CHOOSE LIFE. A man who didn't seem to belong, a leftover radical from the sixties, approached the girls.

"I'm surprised to find someone who is pro-choice at a Christian carnival," he said.

"Oh no, we're not pro-choice; we're pro-life!" they insisted pulling out their sweatshirts from the bottom and smoothing out the letters. "See—CHOOSE LIFE!"

"Wait a minute," he said, twisting his face. "You're pro-life but you want to have a choice in the matter? You still have some thinking to do."

The man walked off and left the girls puzzled, but only for a moment. "Some kind of weirdo, huh?" said one. "Yeah, totally spaced," said another, and then they walked on giggling and bumping into each other, spilling white kernels of popcorn on the ground.

The man was right. These girls had not thought through the implications of their self-proclaimed message. Actually, no one in my dream seemed to have done much thinking about anything. The feelings I had recounting this dream were frighteningly similar to the ones I've had at identical events in real life, and too close to ignore. It was just a dream—but not far removed from reality.

The last scene I remember was a small stage set on the veranda of a large hotel. There was an awning over the stage where a musical group was performing to a very small crowd. Fifty folding chairs were set up, but no more than a dozen disinterested youths were scattered in the back few rows, some leaning back in their seats. They were all dressed in black with punk haircuts. Three were standing and talking as if they were ready to leave. They all looked completely bored.

The people on stage were not only singers and musicians but an entourage of people, well out-numbering the tiny audience. All dressed in early 19th-century costumes, their hair pearl white, they carried themselves with great self-importance.

The women's hair was done in period fashion, with numerous long curls piled high and left to cascade down in the back. A closer look revealed that some of them were wearing wigs made of yarn. Suddenly the yarn stiffened until it turned hard and brittle, and I was staring up at a statuesque porcelain face. It was a beautiful Roman face with perfectly chiseled nostrils and sunken eyes. Then I noticed all the faces were the same, and finally all that I could see, everywhere I looked, was the same sculptured face. It was carved into the tops of the columns that supported the stage, hung above the platform as a large oval medallion where the front of the awning was gathered, and miniaturized in a cameo that graced every neck. The face and the cameo were both the same—sculptured, beautiful, lifeless.

The face was taking over my whole dream. It was a perfect face—beautiful, delicate, and deadly, for it was freezing life and conforming everything to its cold likeness. I remember screaming for it to stop. I picked up a wooden chair and tried to smash the face, and then I awoke to find that it was just a dream . . . just a dream . . . just a dream. . . .

Wasn't it?

ASK
SEEK
KNOCK

QUESTION AUTHORITY

—————6—————

*O*nce in a while you still find it, most likely glued to the bumper of an old beat-up Volvo. It's the popular slogan from the sixties: *Question Authority.* I used to think it was an ungodly statement. I'm not so sure anymore; it all depends on how you read it.

When professional hippie Abbie Hoffman died, the memories and eulogies brought back images of a questioning era. I cannot claim many of those images for myself, isolated as I was by the hedges of evangelicalism. But the spirit of the age affected me just the same.

Three of my four college years were spent at a Christian college. We weren't as radical as students on university campuses, but we did make it tough on the faculty and administration. We asked a lot of questions. During my junior year, however, I attended the University of California at Irvine. It was 1968, the year Robert Kennedy was assassinated.

It was impossible to be on a University of California campus in 1968 and not be affected in some way by the political scene. I wore an R.F.K. button with his initials in the shape of a peace sign, and I had it pinned to my shirt when they told me he was dead. Bobby was the champion of a questioning generation—our hope for changing the system from the inside. I remember exactly where I was when I heard he had been shot, and I still see the picture of his glassy eyes staring up at nothing, disconnected from the life that left its dark flow on the floor around him. I remember thinking along with everyone else, "Oh no, not again!"

Apparently the glue that held the bumper sticker on the Volvo was stronger than the one that held a student movement together in the sixties. When the leaders fell, hope died, and the followers scattered, leaving the bumper sticker to wander on into the seventies and through the eighties, an incongruous slogan against the backdrop of another age with a different perspective. Students today don't question authority. I'm beginning to wish they did.

If "Question Authority" means "don't trust anyone in a position of power," that's pretty good advice. The corruption in Washington and in pulpits across America has shown us the dangerous temptations of power. To question this authority is to keep it honest. The writer of Acts commends the Bereans because they checked the Scriptures daily to see whether the things Paul was saying were in accordance with the truth. To question does not mean to disobey; it means to check it out. The Scripture requires us to do so: Test the spirits, make sure our spirit bears witness to the truth we hear from people in authority (1 John 2:26, 27). "Open mind; pour in" is nowhere on the biblical agenda for the true believer.

And if "Question Authority" means to "scrutinize traditions," this too is good counsel. The value of the Jesus movement of the early seventies was that it brought positive aspects of the radical movement into the church. Why do we have only traditional music in church? Why do we have to wear middle-class clothes and ascribe to middle-class values in order to be in the church? Why do we baptize in the privacy of the church building when the early church always did it in a public place? Why do we have all these denominations? Why do we do things a certain way only because that's the way they've always been done? Do our traditions take precedence over the Bible? Churches that were willing to listen to these questions found themselves joyfully shaken from their dead orthodoxy and infused with a new life and a broader understanding of God and His activity in the world.

Likewise, if "Question Authority" means to "question God," we are right again, because God loves questions. He says He rewards those who earnestly seek Him. He never casts His pearls before pigs; He hides them in parables, in riddles, in questions, so those who really want to know will ask. He wants us to come after it; He wants us to ask why. But no one is asking the right questions anymore.

I find myself on college campuses these days feeling more of a radical than I was as a student, and certainly more radical than current students twenty years my junior. College students simply aren't questioning anymore except the one all-important question: "How will I get a good job and make lots of money?" Social science majors have been replaced by business majors. "Why?" questions have been replaced by "How-to," and Peter Fonda has given way to Michael J. Fox.

I recently taught a course in a Christian college, and I quickly found that many students aren't asking the same questions today as they were in the sixties. My purpose was to make them think, to develop their own ideas, to integrate their faith and apply it— not to regurgitate information I had given out in class.

Some students, however, had a different agenda. They exerted a great deal of energy trying to find out what *I* thought, what kinds of answers *I* was looking for. They didn't want to question "Why?"; they wanted to find out "How?"

The perspective was all too familiar. Many of today's students expect to buy a degree. Their tuition is the purchase price for a professor's knowledge—a series of facts to be put down in their notebooks and be tested on. They purchase information and do not want to be bothered with the side roads of questioning that result in real education.

Rarely do I encounter a student today who is after knowledge and truth for its own sake. College is no longer sought for the widening of one's perspective but for the narrowing of one's abilities toward a specialized job that will translate directly in the economic marketplace. Today, students buy an education in order to obtain a job that will insure a future. To grow, to widen, to investigate, to challenge, to climb an intellectual mountain just because it's there are foreign concepts to this student generation. Methods are more important than meaning. "How?" is more important than "Why?"

The questions being asked today are important because they shape the answers we're getting. They even indicate how we see God and what role He plays in our lives. "How-to" questions narrow into practical answers: steps, plans, methods, formulas. They leave us with specifics and particular things to do, as if life were a true/false, multiple choice quiz. "Why?" questions enlarge our perspective, open up our vulnerability, underline our finiteness, and bring us ultimately to worship God or to despair. To a "Why?" generation, God is the one who is encountered at the end of every question. To a "How-to" generation, God is merely an agent in the process of arriving at a particular goal.

This is not a questioning generation. If it appeared on TV, it's true. If it was shown in a movie, it's accurate. If it came from a person in a place of authority, it's right. Follow the rules, get in, get by, and don't worry about compromise. The system pays, so play the game the best you can; and by all means, don't question authority. These are the slogans of the eighties. I think we could stand a little of the sixties coming around again.

THE AMBIGUITY OF JESUS

—————— 7 ——————

$\mathcal{T}$o read the Gospels is to find the Son of Man free with His questions and careful with His answers. The Gospels read like a riddle. No one today speaks like Jesus.

Jesus always seemed to send people away scratching their heads—even His disciples. He was not a man with easy answers. He was not a seminar leader. He never gave a three-point message; His sermons didn't fall easily into an outline.

Jesus spoke in a way that demanded participatory listening. He did not go the distance to communicate to His hearers. He went so far but no farther, requiring an effort on the part of the listener to meet Him.

His favorite phrase when speaking a public message was "He who has an ear, let him hear." *Hear.* He used it as an activity—something that some people do with their ears, but not necessarily everyone. Apparently a person can have ears and not hear, and in such a case, Jesus is not going to go the extra mile to get that individual's attention. If people find something else to do with their ears, that's their problem. But ears are for hearing, and if there ever was a time for these marvelous instruments to be put to their designed function, it was when the Son of God was speaking.

Jesus had a favorite method of speaking to people. He put it in a story—a parable. When His disciples asked Him why He spoke to the people in parables, He replied: "The knowledge of the secrets of the kingdom of heaven has been given to you but not to them. Whoever has will be given more, and he will have an abundance. Whoever does not have, even what he has will be taken from him. This is why I speak to them in parables" (Matt. 13:11–13).

Thanks, Jesus. That about clears it up. You speak in parables and you answer in riddles. *"He who has . . ."* He who has what? Cars, boats, swimming pools, friends, truth? What does He mean? Now we have two questions: "Why did He speak in parables?" and "What does His answer mean?"

Jesus will not dance on the table for anyone. He doesn't cast pearls before swine. His words demand that we get up, come over, and find out what He's saying. Often we will have to ask more questions about His answers to our questions.

No wonder Luke wrote that the people "hung on his words." He kept them hanging. They either came back for more or they walked away because they didn't want to work that hard.

Jesus' ambiguity points to a most remarkable truth: The One who designed and created the ear gave us the right to use it as we please. He came unto His own, but His own have the freedom to not receive Him if they so choose. Jesus respects His creation.

It had to be this way if He was going to have real fellowship with people. I can only share love with someone who wants to love me. I can only speak to someone who wants to hear. Jesus gave people the room to respond—to come back for more, or to walk away.

To each of His disciples Jesus simply said, "Follow me." That was an invitation, not a requirement. An invitation respects the freedom of the invitee to accept or decline. Indeed, the "no" answer is perhaps the greatest expression of human dignity possible. That men and women can go to heaven is an expression of God's love; that they can go to hell is an expression of the value He places on their freedom.

God desires—not requires—a relationship with us. It is not

42

a one-sided affair; we are co-participants with Him, both in our relationship with Him and in our work in the world.

A woman with a hemorrhage struggled through the press of the crowd in order to touch His garment; four men opened a hole in the ceiling of a crowded house and let down their paralyzed friend in front of Jesus; a centurion soldier asked that Jesus only speak a word so his servant would be healed; a blind man went and washed the clay and the darkness from his eyes; a little boy offered his meager lunch to feed a multitude. Even the miracles of Jesus involved human participation. This was not just a Messianic Magic Show; this was God interacting in human experience—giving and taking, relating with us as Son of Man.

God does not pull all the strings. He counts us as too important for that. To find without seeking, to hear without listening, to say yes without the possibility of saying no is to negate the value of my seeking, my hearing, and my participating. I am not a puppet.

Nor does He put all the pieces together. He leaves holes; He raises questions. He wants me to ask.

QUESTION AND QUESTION
TIME

—— 8 ——

After three days they found Him in the temple courts, sitting among the teachers, listening to them and asking them questions.

—Luke

*O*ne of Gary Larson's "Far Side" cartoons pictures a game show with a moderator and two contestants. One is an ominous bearded figure with streaks of light radiating off his face, and the other, dwarfed by him, is a thin, sheepish looking milk-toast man. Under the glorious figure is the number 684 and under the other, 0. In the caption, the moderator is speaking. "Yes, that's correct! 'Wisconsin' is the right answer! Let's see . . . that makes 684 points for God and for you Norman . . . uh-oh."

We might think that a session with Jesus would be the ultimate question and answer time. If there ever was someone with all the answers, it was Jesus.

However, the picture we see of Christ in the Gospels is far

from "Jesus, the Answer Man." He is, rather, "Jesus, the Answer Dam," holding back knowledge with some; with others, letting measured amounts trickle over its great sloping spillways.

One of His favorite ways to do this was to answer one question with another. With the teachers of the Law, this was understandable; more often than not, they were not truly seeking answers anyway, only wishing to trap Him. But even with His disciples, Jesus often answered their questions with other questions.

When we pull out all these unique questions and answers from the text and look at them together, we come up with a truly enlightening study. But what does the way Jesus answered questions 2,000 years ago have to do with me today?

1. If Jesus dealt with people this way when He was here, what would make me believe He would deal any differently with me now? In place of asking me the question to my face, He allows life to throw the questions at me, forcing me to reach, to find the answers for myself. Life draws my faith out of me, just as these leading questions of Jesus brought forth a true response in those who believed.

Jesus never hands truth to anyone; we must reach out and grasp it. Even when He revealed himself as the Christ, it was always in the context of dialogue; He didn't just drop truth into a person's lap. And at times He even drew the confession out of others with—you guessed it—a question, such as when He asked Peter, "Who do you say I am?" And I, like Peter, must step forward and make a proclamation. Jesus asks me, in some way, to make that step every day.

2. Jesus might allow life to throw its questions at me to trip me up, to upset my apple cart, to smudge my pretty picture before the paint dries, or to topple my delicately balanced stack of blocks—my personal tower of Babel. If I've found security in a system rather than in Christ himself, you can be sure that the gentle probing of His interrogation will sooner or later come and tip the balance on my neat little tidy world.

3. Though I would like to think of myself as exempt from the blindness of the Pharisees, I cannot. Because the blindness of self-righteousness disguising itself as a kind of sight may make me totally unaware of its presence in my life. If this is the case, I can expect my prayers and demands to God to be returned

with the same kind of caustic response He gave the teachers of the law—and thus, I hope, awaken me from my error.

So welcome to the first question and question time with Jesus. It was quite a long and involved press conference with many people present. To simplify our report, we will use the Q. and A. format, identifying, wherever possible, the person asking the question. In every case, the answer (if there is one) will be from Jesus.

Q. (One of John's disciples) How is it that we and the Pharisees fast, but your disciples do not fast? (Matt. 9:14)

A. How can the guests of the bridegroom mourn while he is with them?

————

Q. (Another of John's disciples) John wants to know if you are the one who was to come, or should we expect someone else? (Matt. 11:2)

A. Go back and report to John what you hear and see: The blind receive sight, the lame walk, those who have leprosy are cured, the deaf hear, the dead are raised, and the good news is preached to the poor. [He could have just said yes.]

————

Q. (A Pharisee) Is it lawful to heal on the Sabbath? (Matt. 12:10)

A. If any of you has a sheep and it falls into a pit on the Sabbath, will you not take hold of it and lift it out?

————

Q. (A teacher of the law) Why do your disciples break the tradition of the elders? They don't wash their hands before they eat! (Matt. 15:1)

A. And why do you break the command of God for the sake of your tradition?

————

Q. But your disciples picked grain on the Sabbath. Why are they doing what is unlawful? (Mark 2:24)

A. Have you never read what David did when he and his companions were hungry and in need?

Q. (A Pharisee) Is it lawful for a man to divorce his wife? (Mark 10:2)

A. What did Moses command you?

———

Q. (An expert of the law) Teacher, what must I do to inherit eternal life? (Luke 10:25)

A. What is written in the law? How do you read it?

———

Q. (Someone in the crowd) Teacher, tell my brother to divide the inheritance with me. (Luke 12:13)

A. Man, who appointed me a judge or arbiter between you?

———

Q. (One of the disciples) Where can we get enough bread in this remote place to feed such a crowd? (Matt. 15:33)

A. How many loaves do you have?

———

Q. (One of the chief priests, upon hearing children shouting praises to Jesus) Do you hear what these children are saying?

A. Yes. Have you never read, "From the lips of children and infants have you ordained praise"?

———

Q. (A rich young ruler) Good teacher, what must I do to inherit eternal life? (Mark 10:17)

A. Why do you call me good? No one is good—except God alone.

———

Q. (A Pharisee) Teacher, we know you are a man of integrity. You aren't swayed by men, because you pay no attention to who they are; but you teach the way of God in accordance with the truth. Is it right to pay taxes to Caesar or not? Should we pay or shouldn't we? (Mark 12:14)

A. Why are you trying to trap me? Bring me a denarius and let me look at it. Whose portrait is this? And whose inscription?

Q. (Nicodemus) You have talked of being born of the Spirit; how can this be? (John 3:9)

A. You are Israel's teacher and you do not understand these things? I have spoken to you of earthly things and you do not believe; how then will you believe if I speak of heavenly things?

———

Q. (The chief priests and elders) By what authority are you doing these things? And who gave you this authority? (Matt. 21:23)

A. I will also ask you one question. If you answer me, I will tell you by what authority I am doing these things. John's baptism—where did it come from? Was it from heaven, or from men?

(They discussed it among themselves and said, "If we say, 'From heaven,' He will ask, 'Then why didn't you believe him?' But if we say, 'From men'—we are afraid of the people, for they all hold that John was a prophet." So they answered Jesus . . .) We don't know.

(Jesus) Neither will I tell you by what authority I am doing these things. [They have obviously met their match at this game!]

———

Q. (The Jews, among themselves) How did this man get such learning without having studied? (John 7:15)

A. Has not Moses given you the law? Yet not one of you keeps the law. Why are you trying to kill me?

———

Q. (The Jews) Who are you? (John 8:25)

A. Just what I have been claiming all along.

———

Q. How long will you keep us in suspense? If you are the Christ, tell us plainly. (John 10:24)

A. I did tell you, but you did not believe.

———

Q. (Philip) Lord, show us the Father and that will be enough for us. (John 14:8)

A. Don't you know me, Philip, even after I have been among you such a long time? . . . How can you say "Show us the Father"? Don't you believe that I am in the Father, and the Father is in me?

Q. (The Pharisees) Where is your father? (John 8:19)

A. If you knew me, you would know my Father also.

(At this point in the interview, Jesus decides to turn the tables and ask the first question.)

Q. (Jesus) What do you think about the Christ? Whose son is He? (Matt. 22:42)

A. (Teacher of the law) The son of David.

Q. How is it then that David, speaking by the Spirit, calls Him "Lord"? For he says, "The Lord said to my Lord: 'Sit at my right hand until I put your enemies under your feet.' " If then David calls Him "Lord," how can He be his son? (Matt. 22:43–45)

A. (No one could say a word in reply, and no one dared to ask him any more questions. Instead, they asked numerous unanswered questions among themselves.)

Q. Where does this man intend to go that we cannot find him? Will he go where our people live scattered among the Greeks, and teach the Greeks? What did he mean when he said, "You will look for me, but you will not find me"? and "Where I am, you cannot come"? How can the Christ come from Galilee? Does not the scripture say that the Christ will come from David's family and from Bethlehem, the town where David lived? (John 7:35:36; 41–42)

A. (Various unheard answers of Jesus) Why is my language not clear to you? Because you are unable to hear what I say. Can any of you prove me guilty of sin? If I am telling the truth, why don't you believe me? (John 8:43)

(An observation from one of the temple guards:) No man ever spoke the way this man does. (John 7:46)

———

Q. (Peter, watching Jesus being led away) Lord, why can't I follow you now? I will lay down my life for you. (John 13:37)
A. Will you really lay down your life for me?

———

Q. (Jesus, now before the high priest, is being questioned about His disciples and His teaching. John 18:19)
A. I have spoken openly to the world. I always taught in synagogues or at the temple, where all the Jews come together, I said nothing in secret. Why question me? Ask those who heard me. Surely they know what I said. (John 18:20)

———

Q. (A high priestly official after striking Jesus on the face) Is that any way to answer a high priest? (John 18:22)
A. If I said something wrong, testify as to what is wrong. But if I spoke the truth, why did you strike me?

———

Q. (Pilate) Are you the king of the Jews? (John 18:33)
A. Is that your idea, or did others talk to you about me?

———

Q. (Pilate) What is truth? (John 18:38)
A. No answer.

———

Q. (Then they spit in his face and struck him with their fists. Others slapped him and said,) Prophesy to us, Christ. Who hit you? (Matt. 26:67)
A. No answer.

TRUE BELIEVERS DON'T SWEAR, DARN IT!

—9—

*O*ne winter afternoon I bundled up in my sweats, plugged in my mental tape, and set out to conquer afresh the 1.8-mile jog that has become my necessary touch with the physical—the air, the ground, the pulse, the pain. And today, after a light-snow-followed-by-rain storm typical in this region of eastern Massachusetts, the slush.

These excursions are most appreciated on days like today when a morning of carefully measuring words has left my head feeling thick and slow.

As I concentrated on the rhythmic slapping and splashing of my feet on the watery snow, I could feel the thickness seep from my brain as if the jarring of the pavement had loosened its drain plug and all the weighty thoughts of the day were running down and collecting somewhere around my knees.

Halfway to Hay Street the road curves to the left and rounds a slight hill. On the down side, he was waiting for me—the mortal fear of neighborhood runners, the loose dog who gets his kicks out of chasing moving objects that pass in front of his house. I can't understand how I manage to forget this occurrence day after day until that moment I crest the hill and he first catches my scent or my sound or whatever it is that upsets him so, but I do. This day was no different; once again he caught me by surprise.

This dog guards an imaginary line that extends into the street from either side of his master's property, and treats any intrusion across those lines as an encroachment punishable by a vicious running attack that stops inches short of its prey.

He taunts only, but how can you ever be sure that's all it will be? Once when I was running in California, a dog did nip my leg—luckily getting only a piece of my pants. That experience comes rushing back to my mind every time I try to ignore this menace. What if this is the time he actually goes for me? Maybe some other guy ran by here this morning and swiped at him with a stick and now he's *really* mad!

I have used great restraint in dealing with this problem so far. Ne'er a word has escaped my mouth. I have acted on the assumption that if I ignored him, he would soon tire of this silly game and not bother me anymore. I've kept telling myself each time, *Relax, don't act scared. Animals can sense human feelings. Ignore him, and he'll ignore you.*

But it wasn't working; what's more, my fear appeared to be getting worse. So today as I crested the hill and heard the first warning barks from his sentinel on the porch, I first panicked and then remembered a simple idea I had had last time out. It had occurred to me that he had never yet crossed the street. I go down on his side of the street and come back on the other; so far he's only given me trouble on the first pass. How stupid of me to miss such a simple observation!

So I crossed over and bore down in the slush of the other shoulder, and sure enough, he came only as far as the pavement. *How about that,* I thought. *Why did it take me so long to come up with this?*

Well, we now had a much more relieved and confident runner a few minutes later coming back from his turnaround on Hay Street. But unfortunately, this overconfidence only served to heighten the unexpected nature of the events that were to follow.

As I approached the house, the savage beast began his usual barking two doors down. By the neighbor's yard, he had landed off the porch on all fours and begun his mad yelping dash through the front yard. Not to worry—I told myself. I'm safe as long as I stay over here.

By the time I was even with his yard, however, he was almost in the street, and the sound and speed of his fury blew my safety theory to shreds. *This dog has a target, and it is me! He's coming straight for my legs!*

The well-timed car I quickly hoped for was nowhere in sight—only a flashing, snarling black streak of a dog, hurtling across the street toward my feet. Terrorized, I kept my legs pumping like a machine and my eyes forward. I could not see the slashing mouth at my ankles. I could only hear it, feel its hot breath, and imagine that any second it would be ripping into my supple flesh. Fearing that a violent act on my part would only increase my chances of being bitten, I closed my eyes and used every ounce of composure in me to keep from screaming or kicking him.

But after harassing me two doors past his yard, snapping and lunging at my heels all the way, he finally turned back. My pulse was racing now and my composure left me. All the pent-up fear and anger exploded forth, fueled in its fury by a flammable squirt of instant adrenaline—my mouth opened and I cried out at the top of my lungs:

OPTIONAL ENDING: PLEASE GO TO THE APPROPRIATE CONCLUSION.

1. (Baptists and Independents) "Oh, darn!"
2. (Pentecostals) "Glory to God! Follow the commandment given to us in His Holy Word and subdue this animal!"
3. (Some Presbyterians and Methodists, most Lutherans and Roman Catholics, and everyone who read *Real Christians Don't Dance* and liked it) The same thing that Butch Cassidy and the Sundance Kid said when they jumped off a 30-foot cliff into the Rio Grande.
4. None of the above because true believers don't swear.

WHEN LIFE IMITATES TV

———————10———————

$\mathscr{I}$ often wonder how movie stars handle themselves in real life. The newspaper recently reported that Don Johnson, who plays Sonny Crockett in *Miami Vice*, did just fine. A thief had apparently broken into Johnson's hotel room in Los Angeles and was rifling through his fiancee's purse for jewelry when he was surprised by Johnson and his fiancee returning to their room.

Johnson's well-rehearsed Sonny Crockett role must have clicked right in because, according to the paper, he immediately subdued the guy and held him until hotel security arrived. The officer was quoted as remarking that Johnson had acted fast.

I couldn't help but imagine what this must have been like for the thief. Just think, this guy's going through a routine hotel burglary—he could do this every night with his eyes closed—and suddenly the door flies open and there is Don Johnson (or is it Sonny Crockett?) screaming, "Freeze, pal; Miami Vice!"

You bet he froze! I mean, the guy is in the twilight zone, caught halfway between reality and illusion. "Wait a minute . . . is this Friday night? Did I fall asleep watching the tube? Maybe it's a rerun. Where am I? What the. . . ?"

He's still trying to figure it out when Crockett (or is it Johnson?) gets him face down on the floor, pins his arms behind his back, and begins reading him his rights. Is this life imitating art, or what?

If anything, it's life imitating TV, and I'm sure this goes on in all of our lives a lot more than we realize.

I've watched my children after a couple hours of Saturday morning cartoons trying to get their bodies to BAM! and WHACK! and SPLAT! and ZING! their way through our house. That's when I start looking for body-shaped holes in the walls and order them outside to play.

Our favorite family movie is *Mr. Mom*. We've seen it so many times that we know almost all the lines. In this case, the movie so imitates a lifestyle we already possess that we frequently ping-pong the images from the movie as a kind of family joke. My wife has a high-powered executive job and I'm usually home weekdays, wrestling with home appliances, becoming attached to flannel shirts, and forgetting to shave.

Just last week an associate came to pick up Marti for a business conference, and I had to entertain him while she finished getting ready. I quickly donned my running outfit—a sweatshirt and a silly pair of running pants my children gave me for Christmas that amount to nothing more than a pair of black leotards—and bounded downstairs to let him in.

"You run every day?" he asked, standing gingerly just inside the door with neatly pressed lips and a neatly pressed pinstripe suit.

"Yep. Every day," I grunted, breathing hard and pacing the floor.

"How far?"

"Oh . . . two, three miles. Whatever it takes," I lied. I go 1.8 miles, max.

By the time Marti was downstairs I had instructed him on all the virtues of running that I knew and some that I only supposed while he remained with his back pressed to the front door. As she went out the door behind him, she glanced back at my Peter Pan pants and rolled her eyes in incredulous Terri Garr fashion. I leaned out the door and called out, "Like a little trim on that moustache, Ron?"

These images are harmless; they allow us to look at our lives and mock ourselves, to glimpse for a moment what we must look like to others, and return to our reality a little wiser, taking ourselves perhaps a little less seriously. But such role-play is for those who have a firm grip on reality.

There are times when the line between reality and fantasy becomes blurred, and for some, reality is so oppressive that fantasy is the only escape.

In *Mr. Mom,* when Jack comes out of a daydream sequence based on a soap opera, he realizes he's in real danger, twice removed from reality. It's enough to make him get up out of his easy chair, shave his face, and burn his flannel shirt.

Some people never come out. Some never have reason to.

Would that every thief had a Don Johnson to stop him in his tracks, that every family had a Bill Cosby to diffuse its anger, that every little brother had a Michael J. Fox to look out for his future in the stock market, that every person trapped in a fantasy had a Michael Keaton to kick his shoe through the TV screen. But alas, in the end, these are only images and we must all face our own realities with whatever we have and don't have.

Our lives don't imitate TV. Don Johnson may get his man, but the rest of us end up with the purse swiped. We have to learn to live with the loss, the questions, the feeling that we've been violated—that nothing is safe or sacred when it comes to the real world we live in.

What we have, if we are fortunate enough to have faith, is the Lord. What we don't have is what makes us depend on Him. And even though that may be painful and full of questions, I'll take it over a fantasy any day.

BREAKFAST AT ROSAUERS

—————11—————

*A*cross the street from my motel room here in Spokane, Washington, is a place called Rosauers. It's unlike any place I've ever been. It looks like a supermarket discount department store, but past the newspaper stands, past the check-out stands, the stacks of candy and gum, past the magazine/tabloid rack with its instant promises and inflamed headlines, and the 7-items-or-less express lane, is a "Please Wait to Be Seated" sign and the entrance to a better-than-average family restaurant. K-Mart meets Marie Callender's.

I find myself enchanted, if only by the name. "Rosauers" seems French to me, and this heightens my imagination—which I have recently been putting to work reading the classic French novel, *Madame Bovary* by Gustave Flaubert.

In the novel, Flaubert paints the tragedies of an adulterous love whose passions have been allowed to burn, unbridled, until they consume every living thing in sight. For this, Flaubert was taken to court by the French government in 1857 and charged with immoral and lascivious writing, a threat to public morality.

He was let off with only a warning, thanks to a good defense who proved his novel was actually *valuable* to public morals, an "incitement to virtue through the horror of vice." However appealing an affair might seem, Flaubert's depiction is enough to scare any wife back to her own home. To this defense I add, 132 years later, that it's also enough to scare any husband into putting some passion into his marriage.

My wife certainly isn't complaining. I've been calling her every day from the road, bringing flowers to her office when I'm home, and sending her cards full of sultry love poetry. I just want to make sure there's nobody around who even thinks he can do this better than I. To assume a woman is going to stay true to her husband by virtue of virtue alone is to place a heavy burden on virtue and none on love. Besides, love is a lot more fun.

So as I order hot oatmeal and wheat toast, I imagine I am seated at a sidewalk cafe off a horse-carted street in Rouen, France, having breakfast at Rosauers while writing searing sonnets to the woman I love.

Why must marriage be inversely proportionate to passion? The more married, the less passionate; the more passionate, the less married. In Flaubert's novel, the "banalities of marriage" drove Madame Bovary into her fantasy—and ultimately into the arms of other lovers.

Must life take such a course? Is marriage banal? Was Madame Bovary wrong in wanting more? Must one stay married on virtue alone?

"Café, monsieur?"

"Oui," I say, trying to return to my poetry, but pulled by these questions into other thoughts. Familiarity, routine, kids, responsibilities—are these the death of romance? Is this inevitable?

I read poems of older couples who indicate that the flame of romance inevitably flickers and dies. I wonder if this is what I have to look forward to—only the companionship of two worn-out souls staring into the dying embers of love, fused in their sameness, but ignited no more. Oh, they try to tell me how this older, comfortable-slipper love is much deeper and more fulfilling than the younger, passionate one; but why do I always feel as if they're trying to talk themselves into something they've heard before but don't really believe? Why does it always sound like a resignation?

The waiter comes in with a black tie, brandishing my breakfast of hard roll, butter, marmalade, and hot milk to temper the opaque coffee without losing its heat. I pour the milk from its silver pitcher, stir the steaming mixture, and as I sip the palomino-colored drink, my eyes follow a carriage rattling down the boulevard. The French definitely have a good idea here: hot milk.

Is marriage cold milk to the hot coffee of passion? Some people say it's supposed to be this way. Who could live with the constant intensity a couple gives their relationship in the courting stages? Romance soon gives way to another kind of love, they say, the familiar love of companionship. I know this love. It's roly-poly love. Snuggle love. Care-bear love. It's cute, but it's not my wife and I, and it never will be.

She doesn't want only a friend for a husband; she wants a lover. Maybe other wives aren't like this (I have a feeling they are), but mine is. Suddenly I recognize the similarities. No wonder Madame Bovary gave me such a scare. My wife is Madame Bovary, albeit a righteous one. She's not satisfied with banality. She's too committed to the Lord to find it somewhere else; but if I don't capture her desires, don't understand them and interpret them somehow into our reality, she will be tempted at least toward fantasy.

Love in marriage is not duty; it is an art, and a wise husband knows how to keep his woman happy. To treat marriage as a "catch," to make it the object and the end of the pursuit, is to also make it the end of love. Love is pursuit, and it is never over.

Yes, there is something old about marriage—it builds its own history—but there must always be something new. A static relationship is like ice on a river, mindless of the life that flows underneath. Personalities are never static, and the couple who understand the change will keep heat in their coffee.

Leaving a few francs among the crisp bread crumbs on the clean white tablecloth, I make my way through the iron chairs and out into the street. The city is waking with the sound of vendors pulling up their carts full of fresh produce. Shopkeepers turn signs on their doors, roll their awnings down, and shake the night out of their doormats. Another carriage (or is it the same one?) wanders aimlessly by, an occupied taxi with its curtains drawn—strange for this time of day. I draw in a deep breath of the damp, fertile air that has managed to make its way to my nostrils from the neighboring countryside, and cross the Boulevard Bouvreuil to my room in the Appleton Inn, Spokane, Washington.

Tomorrow I will find out the sad news: Rosauers is a German name.

ROSAUERS REVISITED

——————— 12 ———————

I should have known better. I'm the one who knows German—took three years of it in high school and a semester in college. But I didn't even need that. One need not look beyond "sauerkraut" to see the resemblance. Rosauers is a German name.

So today, Rosauers is a totally different place. The French ambience is gone, replaced by a clean, orderly environment. The rows of shopping goods seem appropriate this morning as I pass by to the entrance of the restaurant. Everything is handy here, right where I need it. What a good idea.

The waitress is cordial but firm, taking me straight to my seat and handing me the menu with a mechanical arm. The food choices are laid out in a logical order, and I find the oatmeal immediately. Today it will come as just that: oatmeal. No surprises. The cafe I imagined the previous day is fading from my memory.

The coffee comes, and I drink it black as I usually do. The oatmeal follows. I like this. Good. This makes sense. Oatmeal. It will keep my cholesterol down.

I get out my yellow legal pad and pen and arrange them neatly in front of me. This morning it happens to be a fresh, new pad, one of my greatest joys. No pages to fold back. No scribbles and slashes of untrimmed thoughts to remind me I don't know all the answers. Fifty empty pages. Waiting.

Today, I will fill them with precise words. I will speak of God and truth in clear sentences. I will lay out the steps. I will make life make sense. This is perfect. They even have extra coffee in a thermal pot. I don't have to wait for the waitress to fill my cup. That makes sense. Everything makes sense.

Except the conversation in the booth next to mine. A very distinguished gentleman is talking to a man half his age in tones too loud to ignore. Seventy is speaking to thirty-five. His voice is lubricated, plausible, obviously well trained in speech, but it has a pleading tone.

I can pick up only pieces, but that is enough. The old man has developed his own enterprise over the years, but it's not a typical business. Something to do with art, theater, maybe even a television show. Whatever it is, he's in the process of dispensing it to the younger, but he has debts and nothing laid up for his future. Seventy is trying to convince thirty-five that what he's selling is not a business, but a lifetime of work. I sneak a glance at thirty-five, and I can tell right away, seventy is not going to get what it's worth.

I resent this. Here I am ready to fill this pad with answers, and I'm presented with a worst case scenario of my own future. Isn't it just like God to dig up my scariest questions and throw them in my face as I was about to write down all the answers?

It's painful to witness this: the old man condescending to the greedy young entrepreneur negotiating his whole life's work for a pot of oatmeal. I suddenly feel the rudeness and disrespect of a system that worships the power of the mark and reduces the sum total of a man's ordered world to a price tag and a plea.

This is no beggar. The man is distinguished. He has his pride. In other cultures and other times not ruled by economics, these roles would be reversed. But this is the 1990s, and the only power anyone respects today is the power of money.

I pull back the top of the coffeepot, and a host of painful questions escape from my subconscious like steam into the air. I pour.

Jesus says you cannot serve God and money, yet money matters seem to permeate almost every decision I make. The Apostle John says that if we have material possessions, see our brother in need, but have no pity on him, how can the love of God be in us? Well, I have material possessions, and I see a whole world in need; but in relationship to the world I live in, I'm only keeping up. Not to mention preparing for the future: medical conditions, elderly parents, college education for the children, retirement. In fact, if nothing changes in my present situation, in twenty-five years I'll be the one sitting in that booth selling my life's work for next month's rent.

The waitress comes by asking if I want anything else. "Nein, danke," I reply. I won't let this happen to me. I won't be where this man is. He's clearly a hopeless romantic paying the price for a life of careless passion. He should have known our system has no sympathy for one who has abandoned Reason for the sake of Art. He should have planned. He should have seen this coming. He should have invested in his future.

I have twenty-five years to set this straight. Providence has interrupted me by this conversation, giving me a look into a future that I still have power to change. Like Ebenezer Scrooge, I've been frightened by the future into a change for the better—only in my case, the change is in reverse. I could afford to take on a little of Ebenezer's former character. After all, one must balance one's books.

I rise to leave, place a few German marks on the clean table, and fold the receipt away in the designated place in my wallet for tax records. I pick up my yellow legal pad—satisfied that appropriate answers have prevailed against this unfair intrusion on its blank sheets—and make my way out through the door to the Badenstrasse. A light rain is falling.

As I step into the street, a carriage appears from out of another century and almost runs over me. A face in the window flashes by with a bare hand brushing away silken hair. It is one face, but at one and the same time, it is all the faces beauty wears—beauty and love and passion and art. "And what of me?" the face pleads. "And what of me?" The carriage rolls on, bouncing and splashing into the enveloping mist, but the face remains in my mind framed by pale, smooth hands on the rear window.

Maybe what is needed here is a wedding—a joining of the two. Either one of these perspectives alone is disastrous. Both the French and the German were smart about this: they gave nouns genders. Everything was either masculine or feminine, and because it was not good for one to be alone, there were weddings going on all the time—almost every sentence.

If I were to reconstruct the English language, I would make certain words feminine: love, passion, beauty, art, freedom; other words would be masculine: logic, control, truth, reason, responsibility. In my language, love would lie down with logic, passion would flow with control, beauty and truth would kiss each other, art would whisper in reason's ear, and freedom would dance with responsibility. As in a good marriage, neither would smother the other, neither would lose identity; on the contrary, each would be enriched and enlivened—in some cases, protected—by the other's presence.

Passion that sees only itself is like a rushing river, dashing those who abandon themselves to it on the rocks of ruin—Madame Bovary. And control that sees only itself dams up the river and settles in. Welcome to Matrimonial Lake, Tepid State Park, Stillwater, Monsieur Bovary's home.

A proper marriage between these two, one with mutual respect, would probably develop a boat—a vessel river-worthy enough to navigate passion's white water and rest in its peaceful pools.

Older couples with successful marriages have learned this. They look at each other's personalities as constantly moving objects against a still background. There is no stagnant water in these relationships. The older man who still loves to look at his wife does so because she is always interesting to him.

And also in my new language, questions would be feminine and answers would be masculine: their marriage, too, would be like a river taking on more significance as it takes on water from its tributaries. More questions, more life, thrown at me from more angles, widens the answer in my experience and deepens the truth.

The eternal marriage between Christ and the believer is, similarly, an ever-widening, ever-growing union. True believers still ask questions because they are an integral part of a living, developing relationship. As in marriage, the union of all of these must remain a mystery if they are to be understood—the face in the window; the pad full of answers; the feminine, the masculine; the questions and the answers; true believers and Christ. The mystery lies always in the joining of the two.

If my reach doesn't go beyond my grasp,
then what's a heaven for,
and for what do I ask?

—Oswald Chambers

PART II

ASK SEEK KNOCK

*Y*ou found it? Good. I did too. So, what now? Is it over?

Is finding the end of seeking? Are there no more yearnings of the soul? Are there only glad songs of victory now as we wing our way homeward? Have I got Him? Does God rest neatly here in my notebook, in my doctrinal statement, in my church, in my point of view?

Or is He still out there at large waiting to reward the seeking heart over and over again? "Seek and you will find"—is that a way in, or a way of life?

Finding is no more the end of seeking than faith is the end of doubt or forgiveness the end of sin.

Some, having found it, will choose to close their minds down

71

over it. Once they have it, they hold it tightly to their chests, let their eyebrows rest darkly on it.

But God is bigger than this. He is capable of showing up wherever He wants. He is the rewarder of those who earnestly seek Him, and seekers know there is still more to be found.

Paul was one of those seekers and he gave us a clear indication that his search was never over—his longing heart never fully satisfied.

"That I may know him . . ." he wrote. Knowing Christ was his driving passion, the motivation for which he was willing to give up everything.

"That I may know him . . ." When did Paul write this? While he was sitting in Damascus waiting, blinded by the revelation of Jesus Christ himself?

Or was it when he was in the desert for fourteen years, hearing directly from God, "consulting no man"?

Maybe it was right before he was caught up into the third heaven, when he didn't know if he was in or out of the body. Or before he was caught up into Paradise and heard inexpressible things, "things that man is not permitted to tell."

No, it was after all that. After the missionary journeys, after the shipwrecks, after the beatings and imprisonments, after so many miracles, after the founding of many churches. While he was in prison in a Roman jail cell, Paul penned this great passion of his soul: "That I may know him. . . ."

If finding was the end of seeking, then Paul would have never written this. And if Paul was still seeking, what does his search say to me?

ASK
SEEK
KNOCK

JESUS IS THE ANSWER

13

Jesus is the answer for the world today;
Above him there's no other, Jesus is the way.[1]
—Andrae Crouch

*O*ne of the most popular songs to come out of the Jesus movement of the sixties was this one by Andrae Crouch. It symbolized a resting place for a restless generation—a clear testimony in the midst of an age of disillusionment. To a culture that had seemingly tried everything and come up short, Jesus was the answer: the peace that was more than a march, the love that was more than a love-in, and the high that was more than hallucination.

Another song from the same period that expressed this Paradise Found had a chorus that went:

Feeling high on the love of my Lord Jesus,
High on the love of my Lord.
And no one's going to tell me, "Chuck it, baby."
'Cause he's my rock and my sword.

My rock: a place to settle after sailing on the stormy seas.

But one generation's answer is often the next generation's problem. To try everything and end up with Jesus is one thing, but starting with Jesus poses an entirely different set of problems. Today, looking beyond the Rock is viewed as a deviation. What happened to the questions, the search, the exploration, the experimentation? The search ultimately led one generation to Christ; now that generation feels the same search will lead their children away from Christ.

How quickly we forget! We allowed ourselves incredible freedoms in our own search for truth, and God was perfectly capable of leading us, in that search, to the knowledge of Christ. But once there, we have a tendency to forget the road home; we want to hurry everyone else along to the answer we've found. If Jesus is the answer, why bother looking? The search is over.

So we bring up our children to acknowledge the answer and close the door on any questions. The end result of this kind of thinking is a narrowing of truth and experience. "Jesus is the answer" for many has turned into a restriction rather than a freedom. Like the Swami character Johnny Carson plays on late night television, Christians hold the envelope up to their heads, close their eyes, and utter the answer: Jesus. No matter what the question is, the answer will always be the same. The question becomes irrelevant. Soon, questioning in general becomes irrelevant, and Christianity becomes a rigid, tight, closed system where the question is viewed as a threat or the evidence of unbelief or lack of faith. We are quick to turn off the process that got us here in the first place.

Jesus never closes a mind: He opens it. Jesus is never threatened by a question: He welcomes it. He knows all questions will ultimately end up with Him, so fire away!

Jesus *is* the answer, and when He walks through a question, He always leaves the door open so anyone can get to it from either side. Modern Christians keep wanting to shut the door (once they've passed through, of course).

For many Christians, the experience of truth has been a narrowing experience, and in one sense this is right. All those questions—religions, sins, frustrations, explorations—finally ended up with Jesus. Like following the inside of a cone, all experiences funneled to a point, and at that point was Jesus on the cross for my sin.

The error, however, is when we stop here and move no further. For our experience of truth to grow, we must move through the cross back out into the same reality—the same questions, the same world—with a different perspective.

It's like an hourglass with the cross at the center. All my pre-conversion experiences narrowed me toward a personal encounter with Christ; but once through, He leads me back out into the world I came from where the lines now, instead of converging, open up into an ever-widening reality. The sands of truth always move this way—in toward the center and out again.

Yes, Jesus is the answer, and it's precisely *because* He is the answer that we can venture out. Because He is Lord of all, we can walk into all and find Him Lord. This is not only a privilege, it's a mandate. It's what Christians are called to do in the world.

———

I have a phobia about balancing my checkbook. I used to think it was because I have a distaste for money. I even convinced myself that dealing with money was handling something unrighteous (ignoring, of course, the fact that Jesus taught me to use money to further the kingdom of God on earth).

After playing a number of spiritual games with this (most of them excuses to avoid responsibility), I finally realized the source of my fear. I hated to balance by checkbook because I was afraid I would find out there wasn't enough money in my account. If I could be assured there was plenty of money, the fear of balancing my checkbook would go away.

If Jesus is the answer, I don't reach the end of my questioning, but a new beginning. I can open the door and rest assured that there's enough truth in this account to cover all the questions I might happen to write. And when it comes time to balance the account, there will always be truth left over.

If Jesus is the answer, then what was that question again?

ASK
SEEK
KNOCK

THE GLORY OF FOOLS

14

It is the glory of God to conceal a matter;
To search out a matter is the glory of kings.
—King Solomon

*T*oday I showed my son how to play the drums. I, player of
guitar and piano, showed my son how to play . . . the drums? I
know perhaps three things about playing the drums, three
things among a thousand, but that's two more than my son
knows, so I showed him how to play the drums.

I took the sticks from him; I sat on his stool; I turned the
music up and played along as best I could. Actually, I'm a frus-
trated drummer at heart; I've always wanted to play the drums.
I hear what I want to play, feel what I want to play—but alas, I
can't play it. Somehow, as I got going, intuition took over and I
actually produced some pretty decent rhythms.

"Like this," I said. "Like this . . . hear the music . . . see, it's
really simple . . . just keep the beat, and once in a while . . . throw

in one of these . . . (CRASH!) . . ." I played on. I wasn't half bad, I thought. And the more I got into it, the more I forgot about my son.

Now a real drummer would have listened to me and heard only three things out of a thousand. But my son, watching from the corner of the room, heard the two things he didn't know yet, and to him, they were like a thousand. I looked up from my fantasy to see my son fighting, in his pride, to hold back the tears; and I realized, too late, what I had done.

I showed him how to play the drums all right . . . I crushed him. I might as well have beat on top of his head with his own sticks; it would have had the same effect. I wonder how long it will be before he gets back on his stool and tries again. Perhaps he'll forget about this. I hope that time and my apology can heal such stupid insensitivity.

All parents must be familiar with those moments when they glimpse in the eyes of their children something forgotten from their own childhood. I remember those tears of frustration. I was the youngest sibling, always trying to catch up with a very competitive family.

I viewed our conversations as a kind of contest. We were not a profusely verbal family, but when we did speak, it seemed to take the form of a race to resolve some issue—to make a point. A question would come up, and there would be a sharp crescendo of discussion until the flag came down and the winner crossed the finish line with the right answer. I remember feeling an abrupt silence following these contests, as if a door had been closed on something wonderful and I couldn't reach the handle. For me at least, the answer, right as it was, had shut me out. I think I felt, in those moments, a little like my son must have felt this morning watching me show him how it's done.

We need not be in such a hurry to race to the answer. We need to allow some time on this side of it—to feel not the abrupt silence after the answer but the pregnant one before. To linger in the question, to hold it, to turn it side to side, end on end, to catch the light on the question's many angles, to see it reflected in each person's perspective, through each person's eyes, to spend a whole evening pushed back from the table, watching the light of truth bounce off all its many faces, is to follow, as a

78

king would follow, the glory of the quest.

Answers are as alive as questions; they grow with experience. The answer is the beginning and the middle as much as it is the end. If Jesus is the answer, then He is to be experienced anew, afresh, in each of our lives—in our doubts, in our dreams, in our questions, and in the silence that sometimes is the only real answer that can follow.

Three simple words will ruin any conversation: "I know that." My seven-year-old uses this trick—it's her favorite phrase. When I am testing her on spelling and correct her incorrect attempt, she will come over and look at the word on the paper to be sure I'm right, and then she'll say, "I know that."

Most people get better at this technique as they grow older. The words need not be said; the effect is known and felt by everyone. It's a downward look from an upturned face, or the wrenching of a body backward after depositing the weight of a heavy verdict, or merely the stiffening of a neck, but it's still said, plainly and clearly, through an impregnable wall: "I know that; I read that book; I know how it turns out."

It is impossible to share a discovery, to give a version of a story or a possible solution to a problem, to bring out one's humble treasure in front of such a person without being crushed.

I wonder how much crushing I've done in my life, how many heads I've beat on like I did my son's this morning? How many times have I assumed people knew nothing about the truth while I knew everything? How many times have I shut the door on someone else's search? How much of this beautiful interplay of light and faces have I missed, waiting to close the curtain on my final act . . . to close, and not to open?

Too often I've looked in the back of the book first, and finding Jesus was the answer, I've closed the book and stopped reading. And I've found the answer crushing instead of lifting, closing instead of opening, dying instead of living. Answers are not dead things that lie inside of books, even the Bible.

If it is the glory of God to conceal a matter and the glory of kings to find it out, then to resolve a matter, to close a case, to shut a door, to end a discussion, to win an argument, to crush a child's first try must be the glory of fools.

I was a fool today. I hope I never forget those tears forming in my son's eyes. I don't want to be one who crushes; I want to lift up.

Answers can be heavy burdens when they're not alive.

"O LOST!"

15

*L*ook *Homeward, Angel* by Thomas Wolfe, copyrighted in 1929, is subtitled: "A Story of the Buried Life." It is a tragic story eloquently told. Almost plotless, it owes its intrigue not to the happening of events but to the desperation of its characters so richly displayed.

Before the first word of this novel, the theme is spelled out in italics on the facing page of chapter 1:

> Naked and alone we came into exile. In her dark womb we did not know our mother's face; from the prison of her flesh we have come into the unspeakable and incommunicable prison of this earth.

> Which of us has known his brother? Which of us has looked into his father's heart? Which of us has not remained forever prison-pent? Which of us is not forever a stranger and alone?

> O waste of loss, in the hot mazes, lost, among bright stars on this most weary unbright cinder, lost! Remembering speechlessly, we seek the great forgotten language, the

lost lane-end into heaven, a stone, a leaf, an unfound door. Where? When?

O lost, and by the wind grieved, ghost, come back again.

Over and over this theme is layered into the lives of one family at the turn of the century. "O lost!" cries from every page in some form or another.

Why would I, who have been found, who knows the One who knew me in the prison of my mother's womb, who has found the unfound door, indeed, the way, the truth, and the life; why would I, who sees life not as a wasted loss, but as a purpose-filled existence touched in ever-widening ways by the hand of God; why would I spend the hours and discipline necessary to drag myself through this painful chronicle of the loneliness and despair of the human soul?

And why not? What right do I have *not* to know this? Do I get to avoid the desperation of human existence because I am a Christian? Is all my lostness lost in being found?

Why do I, who have known the hope of Christ from my childhood, find this story so compelling? Why does some part of me identify with the cries of aloneness represented herein? Is this some sign that I have not been totally found? Or am I being drawn away from my hope by a clever net of the Evil One? Was it a mistake to expose myself to this book in the first place? Should Christians only read stories of hope and victory?

No. For though I am found, I still touch the lostness of my human condition. Though I am found, I still weep at the desperation of man. For I am human. At any given moment, I know what it is to be both lost and found. I hear the cry "O lost!" and I know ... I weep. The minute I lose touch with this is the minute I lose touch with myself in some way.

Jesus wept. He wept for the same reason. For though in His divine nature He knew the power that His Father God had over death, in His human nature He felt the powerlessness, lostness, and desperation of man.

To read the account of the raising of Lazarus is to find Christ entering into the situation almost naive to the human side. He spoke of Lazarus' resurrection matter-of-factly while no one understood Him at all. He spoke of an open door where everyone around Him saw only a wall. It wasn't until He saw Mary and her friends weeping that He was deeply moved in His spirit—as if suddenly all 626 pages of Thomas Wolfe were thrown at Him and He heard the cry "O lost!" And upon hearing it, Jesus wept.

Why was Jesus called "a man of sorrows and acquainted with grief"? Surely if anyone had the right to be hopeful and happy it was Jesus. Unlike us, none of His grief and sorrow was for himself. He had nothing in himself to be sorry for—no burden of His own to bear. No, He walked with the burden of the world on Him. He took on *our* sorrows and was acquainted with *our* grief. He read our story, and the part that cried "O lost!" became His own.

In this same way the story of Thomas Wolfe is my own, too. I know this lostness. I still feel it, for I am still human. To distance myself from this is to deny myself membership in the human race. To distance myself from this is to lose all sense of compassion for my kind. To distance myself from this is to lose something of myself, for though I am found, there is much of my experience that remains lost and found on a daily basis.

Many Christians today have fallen into a trap of focusing on the sin and error of the world. Many have immersed themselves so deeply in this that compassion is far from them. "O wrong!" is the cry of much of contemporary Christianity as it faces the world, when, in fact, the world isn't wrong as much as it is lost. When someone is wrong, you set him straight. When someone is lost, you go out to try to find him as you would a lost sheep, or a lost coin, or a prodigal son.

———

I am not Christ. I bear a small part of the sorrow and grief of the world and unfortunately still, a large amount of my own. I would do well to become more acquainted with the grief of man as well as the hope of Christ, for the truly compassionate Christian is the one who walks the earth as one who is, at the same time, both lost and found.

"Seek and you will find" means even more than I imagined. It includes this novel. In our seeking, we must seek not only the things of God, but we must learn to seek as well the things of man, where God meets us. For in truth, these too are the things of God.

STORIES

——————16——————

*S*he'd been punching it every nine minutes for almost an hour. I could hear the horrid staccato of our alarm clock buzzing, hear it choked off in mid-buzz by the snooze button, and hear the rustling of bed clothes as her body tried once again to find the cherished spot so reluctant to relinquish its warmth to the dark chill of early morning.

I, sweatered and cold-toed in the next room, make my way through the languid streets of Altmont that once lived in the mind of Thomas Wolfe and now lives in the pages of this book— and in my mind, through the power of words. Already 370 pages, and nothing's even happened yet. No one's died. No one's gone to war. No one's even had sex except the fertile earth. In 370 pages, Eugene has simply grown to be 15 years old through waves of fluid description of seasons, lives, and the comings and goings of the ordinary.

The deepest emotions lie skillfully trapped under the surface of this story, an unspoken urge driving it on. That the loneliness of human detachment could be made so compelling is a compliment not only to the story, but to how well it is being told.

But 370 pages and 256 to go? I wonder if I will last. Already on my second renewal, I will wait until the library sends me the yellow notice. The book itself is old, like its writer, and the system, antiquated. The whole experience feels antique, and I like antiques. (No one uses libraries any more than I.) But most of all, the fact that I eventually have to return this book seems an incentive to finish it. Were it mine, I could secure it on my shelf to be finished another day, and Eugene would stay 15 forever.

And I need all the incentive I can get, for in a world of 30-minute sitcoms, 3-second sound bytes, *USA Today,* and *People* magazine, 626 pages of classic literature carries little attraction. But it's growing on me, nonetheless, and as it does, so grows the value of stories.

Stories tell the truth in ways that answers can never tell. Jesus never underestimated the value of a good story. Indeed, all of the Bible, except the epistles of the New Testament, is in some form or another a story. And to think I spent the bulk of my time studying the Scriptures as a young man buried in those few epistles.

We believed the Epistles held the doctrines, the principles of the truth that were illustrated in all the stories. If we could learn the principles, then we could go back to the stories and identify them, and, of course, ultimately work them into our lives so our lives would work. As valuable as this approach may be, I wonder what I missed? I wonder what it would have been like to read those stories without knowing what to look for—without being Sherlock Holmes with a magnifying glass?

Robert Coles, professor of psychiatry at Harvard University, wonders the same thing about his practice in his book *The Call of Stories.* In an attempt to identify a patient's problem, he worries about "messages omitted, yarns gone untold, details brushed aside altogether, in the rush to come to a conclusion."

"Buzz . . . buzz . . . buzz . . . buzz . . . bu—"

I'm going to have to get her up on the next go-round. She'll never make it to work.

At some point along the way, I began to pay attention to women. Women know their stories. They live, talk, and touch them constantly. To a woman, life is a story with which to interpret her own soul in the process of living.

I, like most men, am more likely to miss the story (even my

own) looking for the conclusion, the reason, the answer, even the truth. All these seem so abrupt, so male. Life is female. To pick through life in search of answers only is to miss the story. It's been said that a man can't be a good artist without a well-developed feminine side. I understand that now.

Reading a good story is like listening to a woman—finding out about life. And reading someone else's story can always help me see my own a little clearer.

But stories are best when read alone or told out loud. I worry about a society that sees its stories on TV or the movie screen. There's something to say for the 626 pages I'm wading through right now. Six hundred twenty-six pages of Thomas Wolfe could never be put into two hours and come close to the experience of reading.

This truth was graphically brought home to me in the conclusion to one of my children's favorite movies, *The Princess Bride*. As in a similar movie (another favorite), *The Never-Ending Story*, the viewer is conscious that what we are seeing acted out visually lives in the imaginations of a good book. Perhaps these movie directors understand the literary deficiency of our society and are trying to entice children, hooked on video, with the value and joy of reading.

Intentional or not, the final scene of *The Princess Bride* is all the argument I need. Superimposed for the first time, we hear the voice of the grandfather (who has been reading this story to his grandson), along with the visual enactment of the story, representing the boy's imagination.

On the screen for this final scene is simply—how many times have we seen this—a kiss. But from the book, in the grandfather's ancient voice, we hear something like: "In the history of true love, there have been five truly great kisses, but this one surpassed them all in its purity and its passion."

Now clearly, which one tells more? The kiss on the screen pales when compared to the one I heard in my heart through the words of the story.

"Buzz . . . buzz . . . buzz . . . bu—"

I rush into the room to find her sitting upright in bed, but one hand is searching for the warm spot under the covers. I grab it, slap it, rub it vigorously, and pinch its fingertips. Faint signs of life begin to flow into her face.

"Come on, honey, you've got to get going. Your story awaits you."

"Huh?" she says. Quizzically, she slides off the edge of the bed till her feet jolt on the cold floor, and then she slowly makes her way, robot-like, to the bathroom.

I have a feeling that if Jesus were here today, He would not expect us to show up at a meeting with our notebooks, pencils, and folding chairs. Rather, He would probably seek us out individually, get us alone, and say, "Tell me your story, and I'll tell you mine."

THE ADVENTURES OF REEFER

——————17——————

Author's note: Any resemblance of this story to the Sesame Street children's book *Grover and the Everything in the Whole Wide World Museum* is entirely intentional.

Reefer woke up with the sunlight drenching his face. The ground was still damp from the rain, but the sun felt warm and welcome on his chest. Luckily, he had hung out his other set of clothes the night before. They would be dry now . . . dirty, but dry. He slowly got up, put some water on the Coleman, and lit a cigarette.

Looking out over the sloping hillside, he surveyed the after-birth of a dream. A miscarriage, he thought. All the hopes and dreams of a generation trampled to death in that mudhole that was once Yasgur's Farm. If it was possible to get back to The Garden, one thing was sure now: this wasn't it.

He watched the workers dismantle the scaffolding and wondered if he'd ever hear the music again. High overhead a bomber jet plane rode shotgun in the sky. Two days ago, while on acid, he thought he had seen one of those planes turn into a butterfly, but this morning, on nothing more than caffeine and nicotine, butterflies stayed near the ground where they belonged.

"Where to now, Reefer?"

"I dunno," he shrugged. "Gonna pack my things and walk a long way from here. That much I know."

He walked for two days on back roads, shunning hitchhikers and even friendly advances. He wanted to be alone with his thoughts.

On the third day he heard music. *How can anyone still play music?* he thought. *Don't they know the music died?* As he drew closer he realized this music was different. Somehow different, yet somehow still the same. This music felt peaceful, as if the greatest longing of the soul had found its resolve.

Each step brought him closer until he could hear the lyric of the song. "Welcome back to the things that you once believed in. . . ." The music was coming from what he first thought was a barn, but as he approached it, it grew in size until it became the largest building he'd ever seen. Over the door was a sign: WELCOME TO THE EVERYTHING-IN-THE-KINGDOM-OF-GOD BUILDING.

Oh no, he thought. *Not a good time for this.* He knew he was vulnerable. He didn't want to turn to religion like a rebound from a former lover, but he couldn't deny the appeal. The music was rock, and it was real—like nothing he'd ever heard in church before. And the band playing on the lawn was made up of long-haired freaks just like him, who looked like they'd dropped, smoked, sniffed, snorted, and shot up everything they could get their hands on; but somehow they didn't need it anymore. There was a glow on their faces like a natural high.

The small group that had gathered to hear the music welcomed Reefer as if he were a long-lost friend, and their genuine love soon won over all his fears. Reefer was a lost cause. His needy, thirsty soul drank up every drop of living water he could get into his cup. After being softened by the music, he was ushered into the huge building, where he spent the first days and weeks in a state of complete spiritual euphoria.

In short, Reefer fell in love with Jesus. For several years he moved from room to room in this huge building, finding out more and more of the wonders of the kingdom of God.

But that was twenty years ago; now, once again, Reefer is restless. In twenty years, he's been through so many rooms in the EVERYTHING-IN-THE-KINGDOM-OF-GOD BUILD-ING that he wonders if there is more. Each time he moved from one room to the next, he had been surprised to find the building grow.

First there had been the Born-Again Room where he was baptized and educated in the elementary doctrines of the Christian faith. He spent the most time in this room (over seven years), and left his fondest memories there. His favorite duty, though it was hardly a duty to him, had been to sing to the streets out in front of the building where he'd first seen the band. He loved watching the disillusionment on so many faces turn to joy, and his greatest thrill had been bringing some of his old friends to Jesus.

But after seven years, the room had started to get crowded, and Reefer wanted to move on in his Christian life. Fortunately he found out there were more rooms in this building than the Born-Again Room.

Someone invited him to the Second-Blessing Room. Here he learned there was more to being a Christian than just being saved. He learned to praise God as he'd never done before. Coupled with this room was the Rapture Room. It had a big Rapture Clock on the wall and daily seminars on latest scholarly updates concerning the return of Christ. Reefer spent a couple years in these two rooms praising Jesus and longing for His return.

After all those seminars on prophecy, however, Reefer had begun to notice a growing hunger for the Word. He realized there was so much he didn't know. Fortunately he found the Discipleship Room, where he immersed himself in a detailed study of biblical truth. There were seminars, notebooks, textbooks, lectures, small group discussions, weekend retreats; and Reefer soaked up everything he could get.

But the next room was his biggest surprise. Reefer had no idea such a room could exist in the kingdom of God. He actually spent a great deal of time in this room until he realized where he was. He had simply overdosed on spiritual truth—he took in more stuff in the Discipleship Room than he could ever possibly use—and fell squarely into the Apathy Room in the basement, where he wallowed for some time.

He found out, though, that even this was part of God's plan. There in the basement, Reefer had discovered that Jesus was still with him even if he didn't feel Him. By the time he left Apathy Room, he was actually thankful for having gone through this experience.

But he was also excited about the next room: the Renewal Room. Reefer was ready. This was to be the most exciting time for him since the Born-Again Room. He loved the planning and the preparation that went into going back out on the streets to spread the news of the kingdom. They talked renewal; they talked about exploding evangelism; they talked about taking it to the streets. Reefer couldn't wait to get going, but then something horrible had happened. After all their training and preparation, they never made it to the streets. It seemed they had come so far into the building that no one knew how to get out.

Now Reefer has reached his lowest point in twenty years. He's presently bored to death drinking Christian non-alcoholic beer in the Christian Culture Room. Unable to find their way back to the world, all the Christians have decided to create their own version of the world where they can be Christians and still enjoy as much as they possibly can of the world. To Reefer, this is like one big decaffeinated experience. There are TV monitors with three Christian networks playing at once. Christian aerobics are being held continuously in one corner. There are Christian music listening stations everywhere, and Christian theater playing in another corner. The place is swarming with chiropractors, nutritionists, body builders, fashion experts, color consultants, psychologists, lawyers, doctors, and professional people of every kind—all operating strictly for Christians in the kingdom of God.

Reefer sits on the floor, leaning against a red and white banner that resembles a Coca-Cola ad. Only this one reads: Jesus Is the Real Thing. He thinks back to that day twenty years ago when the music died. Sadly he listens to all the music blaring in this room and realizes that it sounds just as dead as the old music. In fact, the old music actually seems better in his memory, for at least it was honest. It was about a dream that failed, but it was a real hope. This music is about a dream that he knows has come true, but the way it expresses that hope fails to convince him.

His spirit cries out from within him, "God, is this it? Is this all there is in your kingdom?"

Unable to help himself, Reefer picks up his guitar and starts singing one of those old songs that seem strangely appropriate: "Bye, Bye, Miss American Pie."

Suddenly Reefer stops. He feels a draft on the floor behind him from underneath the Jesus Is the Real Thing banner. *What can this be?* he wonders. Crouching low to see under the banner, he discovers what looks like a crack made by the bottom of a door. Squeezing behind the banner, he finds not only a door but an unlocked door—something he hasn't found in twenty years in this building. All the other doors have doorkeepers.

Reefer quietly slips into the next room and discovers a musty old back room full of theater props, podiums, choir robes, broken pinball machines—most of the stuff no longer in service. There is no light on in the room; he can see, but barely. He searches to find the source of light and discovers, to his amazement, that it's coming from under two big double doors in the opposite wall.

Reefer recognizes it immediately as sunlight. These doors go outside! Trembling, he gingerly pushes the long handle and the doors swing open, bathing him in blinding sunshine. It's been twenty years since he's seen the outside world.

Slowly, as his eyes adjust to the light, he begins to make out the ridge of a hill opening into a wide valley. A stream runs through the middle of the valley, glistening in the sun. And beyond the stream, through a hazy sky, he can see the faint outline of a city. It all looks so good to him . . . even the smog. He wants to open his heart, to shout, to sing; but suddenly his mind grips down on this freedom, holding it hard and throwing it to the ground before him.

How can I feel this way? My heart belongs to the Lord, yet it's leaping at seeing the world outside. He stands frozen in the doorway. He thinks of his old friends—all the people he's lost touch with. He wonders how God could allow his heart to long for something his mind tells him is wrong.

He looks up and cries, "God, speak to me! What are you trying to say? Why do I feel so torn? How can I go back inside when I feel as if you're calling me out? But how could you call me out of your kingdom? Whose voice is this, God? Speak to me. Speak to me."

His eyes open from his prayer and immediately fall on something he didn't see before in the faint light of the room—there, over the door. It's a sign like all the other signs over all the other doors in this building. *These double doors to the outside have been labeled.* Reefer can make out a few letters, but with all the dust and cobwebs, the whole title is unintelligible.

Quickly he piles up a couple of wooden crates, finds a broom, and scrambling up, begins brushing off the sign over this unused exit.

What he uncovers brings unspeakable joy and resolve to his torn heart. In an instant, God has answered his prayer.

The sign simply reads: EVERYTHING ELSE IN THE KINGDOM OF GOD.

G CHRISTIANS IN AN R-RATED WORLD

—————— 18 ——————

$\int$ ooner or later Christians are going to have to face the fact that the world we live in is R-rated, and contrary to prevailing Christian opinion, our job is not to try to change that R to a PG.

We are so selfish. We want the world to change for our benefit so we don't have to be uncomfortable. Never mind a person's eternal destiny; just don't submit me to a dirty joke: it's too embarrassing. I know we think like this because I've been trained in this kind of thinking.

If Jesus had treated us the way we treat the world, none of us would stand a chance of being saved. Romans says that while we were yet sinners, Christ died for us; remember what He said from the cross? "Father, forgive them, for they know not what they do." Jesus didn't let our sin get in the way of His love. He carried that forgiveness all the way to His own cross. Christians will find a similar cross waiting for them if they are going to love the world as He did.

Paul says we are ambassadors of reconciliation to the world: we are on a mission to bring people back to God. A key element in that process is not counting people's sins against them any longer (2 Cor. 5:19). This is the glorious good news: God has removed the barrier between himself and me, that is, my sin. I sing with that great hymn writer:

> My sin, oh, the bliss of this glorious thought,
> My sin, not in part, but the whole,
> Is nailed to the cross, I bear it no more,
> Praise the Lord, Praise the Lord, oh, my soul!

Joe at work swears, cheats on his wife, and brags about it. Are his sins nailed up there too? You better believe it! And this is where we get tripped up. If Jesus removed the barrier separating himself from sinful people, and I'm still encountering one between myself and unbelievers, there can be only one person putting it there—me. I'm happy to have that barrier removed for me, but not for anyone else.

"But, Jesus, the guy's obnoxious! You can't expect me to love him, can you?" I can hear myself say it, and I can hear the Lord's reply, "How do you expect me to love you? How do you think you look to me without the cross, where I removed your sin from me? Take the telephone pole out of your own eye, and you will be able to see him as I do."

The gospel pleads a message of grace, and still Christians live as if they are G people offended by an R-rated world. If I find unbelievers objectionable, I can be pretty sure I haven't done adequate business with my own sin.

In fact, the way I feel about being around unbelievers will tell me a whole lot about my concept of God and how I stand before Him. Jesus put it this way: "Do not judge, or you too will be judged. For in the same way you judge others, you will be judged, and with the measure you use, it will be measured to you" (Matt. 7:1–2).

In other words, you get what you give out. You want a loving God? Then be loving. You want a merciful God? Then be merciful. Want God to forgive you? Then forgive your fellowman. Want God to condemn you? Then be an accusatory person. Want to put yourself above the rest of the world? Then get ready for a God who is going to strain out every judgmental thought you've ever had and measure all the thoughts and intents of your hidden heart by the same standard.

That's enough to send me to my knees, because I know my heart. You and I as Christians need to realize that however acceptable our lives may be for the general audience, we still possess an R-rated heart, and we're as good as dead if we want God to meet us on any other ground than His grace and forgiveness.

The joy of this truth is that once I can believe that forgiveness for myself, then I can believe it for anybody. I have new eyes to see beyond my neighbor's sin and love him or her with the love of Christ.

When we search the Gospels, we never find a place where Jesus was offended by a sinful person. But there are repeated accounts of His being offended by the self-righteousness of so-called holy people who set themselves apart from the rest of humanity in their own eyes. For these people, He didn't even have the time of day, except to warn them of the judgment to come, a judgment brought about by their refusal to see themselves as needy as the next guy.

IN THE DIRT

19

*H*e was just getting ready to teach in the temple courts. His popularity was at a peak among the people and begrudged among the religious leaders. All Jesus had to do was sit down in the court—a customary sign that a teacher was ready to teach—and a crowd would gather to listen.

This time, however, before He could even begin, a disturbance worked its way from the back of the crowd to the front as the teachers of the law pushed and shoved their way to where He sat. One of them was gripping a woman, twisting and turning in an exhausted attempt to free herself from him. Reaching the front of the crowd, he flung her into the center of the circle where she staggered to a standstill. The crowd pressed in for a closer look; the woman, trapped and humiliated, looked up at the sky and then down at the ground, wringing her arms as if to rid them of the man's touch.

"Teacher," said one of them, hot-breathed and hungry; they knew they had a double kill this time—the woman *and* Jesus. As for calling Him "teacher," that was pure mockery, for they were about to prove Him otherwise. "This woman was caught in the act of adultery. In the law, Moses commanded us to stone such a woman." He emphasized the word "such" as if it gave him pleasure. "Now what do you say?"

Jesus, still seated, stared at the men, then at the woman who was studying the ground, rocking nervously, and then He too looked down, bent over, and began to write something in the dirt.

The Pharisees surveyed the scene smugly. They had Him in a corner, and He wasn't even coming out! Like a pack of wild animals toying with a wounded prey, they pressed Jesus for an answer. But He went right on writing on the ground. The woman chanced a glance in His direction, amazed to find herself not the only victim of this situation. Jesus, ignoring all, went on writing in the dirt.

Why? Was Jesus at a loss for words? Did He need time to gather His thoughts? What did He see in the dirt? What did He write?

No one knows. No one needs to know, or we would have been told. What we do know is that this strange diversion was an important part of the drama. At no loss for words, Jesus was waiting for the time when His words would mean the most. The teachers of the law thought they had Him; when, in fact, they were the ones being drawn into the net.

I can't help thinking that in those moments, as Jesus fingered the dust of the ground, He was rummaging through the common element of humanity that He saw there: "For dust you are and to dust you will return." Looking at the people in this drama, we see the apparent righteousness and unrighteousness of men. Looking down, we see common ground—the weakness and frailty in everyone. Out of that common clay of universal guilt, Jesus finally straightened up and spoke the words that forced a personal encounter with truth for everyone who heard: "If any one of you is without sin, let him be the first to throw a stone at her."

Suddenly righteousness and self-defense turned to dirt in the mouth, and one by one, the dust of departing feet rose and fell back to earth.

And what was Jesus doing during this exodus? Was He watching, gloating, viewing with pleasure the turnabout He had wrought with one well-placed sentence? No. He didn't see a thing, for He immediately went back to work on His diary in the dirt—this mysterious earthbound exposition.

Only this time it was even more significant, for He left the Pharisees to ponder His words. He delivered His verdict of truth and then removed himself from the situation.

Jesus knew what the outcome would be; He didn't have to watch. He would talk to whoever was left—whoever was ready and willing. He always allows people the right to come to their own conclusions. No one can be forced to learn before he is ready.

Who knows how long the woman stood there watching Him bent over, busy in the dirt? She could have gone too, but she didn't. Something about Him held her. Perhaps she was ready. Finally Jesus straightened up again and, as if returning from some faraway place, spoke to her. "Woman, where are they? Has no one condemned you?"

"No one, sir," she said.

"Then neither do I condemn you. Go now, and leave your life of sin."

Jesus, the only one who was without sin, the only one ever with the right to throw the first stone, didn't.

Instead, He wrote on the ground.

And He continues to write in the dirt of every life that stands before Him accused. He holds no stones; instead, He is a master artist capable of working with the most earthbound of mediums.

He is practiced in the art of working with the dust of the ground, so He can bend over and write the most beautiful stories on the dust of a life—your life, my life—any life, that is, that doesn't walk away.

THE GOSPEL (RATED R)

———————— 20 ————————

I have a feeling that if someone made a movie of my life and they made it honestly, it would have to receive an R rating. As much as I would like to get it to a PG or at least a PG–13, I would have to sacrifice a certain amount of realism and truth-telling to do so.

The fact is: life is R-rated. There just aren't PG or G people running around. If you told the whole truth about anyone, you'd have to restrict audiences: Under 17 not admitted without accompanying parent or adult guardian.

The issue is not what I've done or thought about doing; it's what I will *admit* to having done or thought. Every time I write about myself, especially what's behind the self I project, I have to decide how much truth I'm going to tell. How much shall I divulge? Shall I give them the full-length feature film or the edited-for-television version? The distance I go with this will determine the movie rating on my life.

John Sayles describes his movie *Eight Men Out* as the story of the first true confessions of American sports. "America lost its innocence long before 1919, but didn't *admit* it, especially in sports," he says in a *Boston Globe* interview. The movie tells the story of a handful of Chicago White Sox players who became known as the Black Sox by taking gamblers' payoffs and throwing the 1919 World Series. "Sports writers were writing this incredible purple prose about 'our boys on the field,' " Sayles says. "They never mentioned that they dragged some of those boys out of a bar throwing up at four in the morning. It wasn't innocence that was lost, but the ability to *look* on ourselves as innocent."[1]

Yes, America *did* lose its innocence long before 1919. America lost its innocence long before it was America.

Man lost his innocence in The Garden.

The serpent was right. "God knows that when you eat of (the fruit), your eyes will be opened, and you will be like God, knowing good and evil."

"Like God" in that you will know more than you know now—knowing both good and evil. But you will not be "like God" in your ability to do anything about it. What the Enemy didn't tell the woman was that good and evil were more powerful than she. Having her eyes opened would put her in a chasm between the two, in the place of decision, but without strength enough or intelligence enough to choose good every time.

It was that knowledge that turned the innocence of a G-rated garden experience into an R-rated reality. Adam and Eve immediately lost the ability to look upon themselves as innocent. Though they had been naked and unashamed, now they knew their nakedness; and for the first time they were conscious of self and of its power to use and to abuse. They saw at once the beauty and the terror of each other and their own intentions.

We all are born with this same knowledge. We know the good and long for it; we know the evil and fear it—in ourselves and in one another. Each life story is a chronicle of choices and the interplay between good and evil. If I play it all out on the screen, I must cover myself, restrict my audience, protect the rating. I don't choose good all the time. I don't always even recognize what good is. Let's face it, life is not suitable for general audiences.

---

[1]Jay Car, "Sayles' Eight Men Out—Rich, Evocative, and On Target," Sept. 21, 1988. Reprinted courtesy of *The Boston Globe*.

But thank God, neither is the gospel. "You see, at just the right time, when we were still powerless, Christ died for the ungodly. Very rarely will anyone die for a righteous man, though for a good man someone might possibly dare to die. But God demonstrates his own love for us in this: While we were still sinners, Christ died for us" (Rom. 5:6–8).

My sin. Christ's death. Not exactly stuff for the Disney Channel. But this is the whole point. A Disney gospel would never reach me where I need to be reached. Tinkerbell flying through the air to the Magic Kingdom every night at nine followed by fireworks is not the kind of gospel I need.

"While we were still sinners, Christ died for us." If my life is R-rated, then so is the gospel, because Christ meets me at my worst. He meets me naked and ashamed and covers me with His forgiveness. He has seen this movie—every scene, every detail—even the stuff I can't put into this book. He took it all in. He who knew no sin *became* sin for me. *The Last Temptation of Christ* was not the half of it. He has seen every blasphemous movie ever made, every life ruined, every innocence lost. He took all that on himself, embraced its ugliness, and then He died, putting it all away forever.

I don't want the edited version of this gospel. I don't want the one suitable for TV or in-flight programming. I want the first run, full-length feature presentation of this gospel—the one that shows all of my life and all of His and the inexplicable joy of His forgiveness. (Rated R.)

ONWARD,
CHRISTIAN SOLDIERS

21

Onward, Christian soldiers, marching as to war, with the cross of Jesus going on before." As this traditional hymn indicates, militarism has played a major role in the history of the Christian Church. Its roots go all the way back to the battles of the children of Israel against pagan Canaanite nations. Most of David's writings in the Psalms are war-related.

The New Testament picks up the theme with Paul's injunction to "put on the whole armor of God" and "fight the good fight of faith." He often called himself and his colleagues in the ministry "soldiers of Christ."

Today in the Christian Church we see many evidences of militarism. The Salvation Army and Boys' Brigade are highly developed organizations that rely heavily on a military theme. These themes have played major roles at times in the contemporary Christian music of Russ Taff, Petra, DeGarmo and Key, and the Allies, and at least minor roles in everyone else's—myself included. There is hardly a sermon, concert, or Christian talk show today where the spiritual battle cry is not sounded in some way.

The fact that spiritual conflict is a reality in a believer's life cannot be disputed; but equally undisputable is the fact that Christian militancy can also be misguided and abused. The huge injustices of the Holy Wars of the Crusades; the Salem witch trials; the religious wars in Ireland—each side claiming a spiritual vendetta; the Christian militia in the Middle East; and the abortion clinic demolitions in our own society—all give the old hymn a new twist: "Onward, Christian soldiers, marching as to war, with our own agenda going on before."

There should be a big sign on the door as Christians walk into the armory of military words, phrases, and images: DANGER: HIGH EXPLOSIVES; EXERCISE EXTREME CAUTION.

On the surface, the conflict seems like a simple battle between good and evil, truth and error, right and wrong, with little Johnny Christian standing in the middle trying to fight for all that is good, true, and right in the world. But life is actually a far more complicated, layered reality than this picture would indicate. Is Johnny Christian good all the time? Does Johnny Christian always know what is right? Is he sure he's found the real enemy? Is Johnny Christian defending himself or the truth? And what's to keep Johnny Christian from using spiritual warfare as a way to legitimize his personal prejudices—which, in fact, are the real evil he's supposed to be fighting?

Mass self-righteousness is a terribly dangerous and powerful force. Hitler built his regime on it. Cries of "We're right and everyone else out there is wrong. We're gonna win! We're gonna be vindicated! God is on our side!" can create an emotional blind that masks an evil greater than if evil were personified. No one dedicated to the Nazi cause felt themselves supremely evil; on the contrary, they were convinced that everything they were doing was for the cause of something supremely good.

I wonder about a Christian community that has become more concerned with being right than being loving—more concerned with winning than caring. Christians seem to be in a contest with the world to prove that they are better: Christians have more fun, better marriages, more love, more success and better coping power than the world.

The extent to which Christians actually feel they are in a contest with the world is the extent to which a wedge is being driven between them and the world. When this isolation is compounded by the embarrassment of the highly publicized Christian TV empire and its resulting ridicule in the press, the result is a very maligned, defensive group of people hoping for some kind of retribution—fertile ground for fighting words that lead into the wrong battle.

But the real tragedy is that Christians who take a defensive stance against the world are losing a sense of the reason for their existence here. The good news of God's love for the world through Jesus Christ is being eclipsed by the bad news of a self-declared Christian war against the world.

In truth, we are *not* at war with the world. Jesus Christ did not come to declare war on secular society; He came to save it. Nor did Jesus save Christians so He could show the world how much better off the believers were. He saved us because He loves us and wants a relationship with us. He wants that same relationship with everyone. "For God so loved the world that he gave his one and only Son, that whoever believes in him shall not perish but have eternal life. For God did not send his Son into the world to condemn the world, but to save the world through him" (John 3:16–17). Do these familiar verses sound like a battle cry?

We need to send a different message to the world than the one we're giving. Paul says that "God was reconciling the world to himself in Christ, not counting men's sins against them. And he has committed to us the message of reconciliation" (2 Cor. 5:19). We're getting mad at the world when God has told us clearly that He wants us to tell the world that He isn't mad anymore. Is anyone confused here? If God isn't mad at the world, why are we? If He isn't counting sins against people any longer, perhaps it would be a good idea for us to throw away our record book as well.

So what happens to Christian warfare? We have to make sure we're fighting the right war on the right battlefield. Scripture tells us we are at war with spiritual forces and rulers of wickedness in heavenly places, and the battlefield is in our own minds and hearts where we fight temptation, doubt, and the lies of Satan. Jealousy, envy, selfishness, slander, depression, despair, unbelief—these are the darts the Wicked One throws at us. God intends us to fight the very things that are crippling the Christian Church, that are presently being justified by the wrong war with the wrong enemy—things like pride, prejudice, supremacy, and self-righteousness.

Actually, the old hymn was right all along. "Onward, Christian soldiers, marching as to war, with the cross of Jesus going on before." If I take the cross of Jesus into battle—the same one He had me pick up when He asked me to deny myself and follow Him—then my pride, prejudice, and right to be right are hung there, too. From this same cross Jesus looked out at the world that was crucifying Him and said, "Father, forgive them, for they know not what they do."

If I go into battle with any other cross before me, I am not a Christian soldier.

THE BIG FAITH

22

$\mathscr{I}$ frequently hear a complaint that has a way of laying more bricks on an imaginary wall that already separates Christians from the world. I've used it often myself. "I really don't talk to non-Christians very much because we have so little in common. They have no interest in spiritual things. What is there to talk about?"

The danger of this complaint is that it sounds so holy. We are so taken with our own spiritual aura that to have to spend an inordinate amount of time discussing things like the weather, politics, TV, or baseball is demeaning to our higher sense of revelation. It appears noble indeed until you realize that we spend most of our time with other Christians discussing nothing more than the weather, politics, TV, or baseball. What we really don't want to have to encounter is not some unspiritual subject but another point of view.

J. B. Phillips said it years ago in the title of his classic book: *Your God Is Too Small.* Many Christians have simply drawn a line, a circumference around themselves and their God, beyond which truth does not exist. Once the sanctity of this little sphere is captured, they guard it, defend it, protect it, and reluctantly venture outside of it only when necessary. Most Christians today are not seeking and finding; they are too busy hoarding and defending what they already found. If this is truly the extent of one's faith, it is a small faith, indeed.

The Big Faith ventures out with nothing to fear. The Big Faith believes that God can be found just as easily in the public library as in the church's. The Big Faith finds truth in art and in culture, in politics and on TV, even in the weather report or at a baseball game. The Big Faith can walk into almost any conversation and knowledgeably help point it toward the truth, if it wasn't already pointed in that direction in the first place. The Big Faith believes everyone knows *some* truth and is able to start with what they know and connect it carefully to Jesus.

Truth is not an exclusive personal possession of Christians. Truth is woven into the fabric of the universe, and The Big Faith will seek it out and find it wherever it is to be found.

The Scriptures even tell us that a good deal of man's artistic expression, regardless of the knowledge of God, is, in essence, a longing for eternal destiny—a thirst for spiritual things. "I have seen the burden God has laid on men. He has made everything beautiful in its time. He has also set eternity in the hearts of men; yet they cannot fathom what God has done from beginning to end" (Eccles. 3:10–11).

Is this not an ideal description of artistic frustration: eternity in one's heart, and yet a finite mind? I walk into any art museum and find this desperation flung on every wall. In finding and identifying this frustration, a believer with The Big Faith will be finding truth.

For truth is not only found in the answers. Much of art, though lacking in answers, may succeed in asking the right questions, and this too, is part of truth.

In the climax of the movie *Bladerunner,* Harrison Ford is saved from the brink of death by a human "replicant" (a robot) who up until that time had been his archenemy. Ford, bewildered by this strange turn of events, then watches the "replicant" terminate (die), and thinks out loud, "I'll never know why he saved my life. Perhaps in his last moments he realized it was life he was after . . . my life . . . anybody's life. Maybe he was only seeking the answers to the same questions we all have: Where did we came from? Where are we going? How long have we got?"

I've viewed this scene five or six times, and never once have I failed to be deeply moved. It reaches into the deepest questions of the human soul, questions that will ultimately lead a person to God or to despair, and it is not afraid to shout them from the screen. Indeed, the whole movie was made to display these three questions in a powerful, dramatic context. Eternity in the heart, coupled with a finite mind, leaves us with questions—but at least they are the right questions.

In his play *St. Joan*, George Bernard Shaw has used the historical character of Joan of Arc to express the same frustration. Joan's heart for God and for the people of France is simply too big to fit into the finite structures of the state and the church. A mere teenager, she dies at the stake for the crime of having too big a faith—an eternal heart crushed by finite minds.

The popular singer/songwriter Sting, when he was with the rock group Police, wrote and performed a song entitled "Message in a Bottle." In it he expressed the eternity in his heart as an SOS to the world that he sent floating away in a bottle. Returning days later, he found a hundred million bottles cast upon the shore and realized that he was only one of millions of castaways seeking a home—an eternal heart, trapped inside a bottle, clanking up and down against so many other imprisoned souls, bobbing in a sea of loneliness.

These kinds of discoveries await the true believer with The Big Faith—out beyond the small circumference where "Christian" is only an adjective. For the most part, the discoveries will strike with pain and with compassion. They will awaken a true evangelistic heart (as opposed to "witnessing" as a rung on a spiritual ladder) and remind us of the image of God that still hangs on every face and reflects in the window of every personality. They will illuminate the eternal glory and the everlasting horror that are the potential of every soul. And they will put into the believer the heart of God, who is not willing for any to perish but for all to come to repentance.

True believers with The Big Faith will be able to walk out into the world and not lose their faith. They will not have to depend on labels to make their world secure. They can even join hands with the world in support of those things that they know

Jesus would support—justice, mercy, human rights, feeding the hungry, caring for the poor and the oppressed—for Jesus himself said, "He who is not against you is for you."

"This Is My Father's World" is a famous hymn sung often in churches today. The Big Faith believes it is true, and looks at all the disciplines of the world in this light. To study science, art, philosophy, and the humanities is to look into the realm of God in all things.

Frank E. Gaebelein (1899–1983), founder of Stony Brook School and respected author and editor with *Christianity Today* and the New Scofield Reference Bible, loved to call himself a "Christian humanist." This label would not be a popular term today with Christians at war with secular humanism, but there was nothing secular in Gaebelein's humanism. He was talking about bringing the knowledge of God to light in all human disciplines, and he founded a school dedicated to that purpose. He took seriously Paul's statement to Titus: "To the pure, all things are pure," and ventured courageously into the kingdom of men to find the kingdom of God. Frank Gaebelein was a Christian Renaissance man; he had The Big Faith.

The rise of secular humanism in our society is not so much the result of Christians losing a war with the world as it is evidence that Christians have in large numbers abandoned the world. Where are the leaders and volunteers in society who, as true believers, can represent a *sacred* humanism in the world by their values, their love, and their hard work? The Little Faith runs away from the world, blaming secular humanism for every ill. The Big Faith runs into the world with healing power of the love of Christ.

Why do non-Christians have an impression of Christians as people who are boring, bigoted, and narrow-minded? Could it be true? Could they be right? Those Christians for whom the accusation is true have become disinterested, unattached, and illiterate when it comes to the things that go on in our world. Their God is too small. Jesus said the way that leads to life is narrow, but He never said the mind that follows the way had to be narrow as well.

Too many modern Christians have taken the fact that "Jesus is the answer" as an excuse from school. The mind is already made up, awareness is shut down, and everything is looked at with a preconceived eye.

The Big Faith has an open eye, an open mind, and a wide angle on truth; class is always in session. True believers are fascinating people, always searching and growing in their knowledge of God and His presence in the world. They do not limit the domain of God to something they understand and control. Christians who walk out into the world with The Big Faith always discover when they get there that, much to their amazement, God got there first!

ASK
SEEK
KNOCK

11B
——— 23 ———

*A*ny seasoned traveler should be well acquainted with the sinking feeling associated with first discovering that he or she has been reluctantly assigned a B or an E seat for a three-hour flight. I'm a C-D person myself—most comfortable with the aisle seat. Even if the plane is full, I still have one open side and free access to the lavatory without having to crawl over any bodies.

With travel agents routinely preassigning seats, this usually gets taken care of; but occasionally plans change or computers break down, and I sometimes have to suffer a B or an E seat. And you can be sure, if you are 11B, that all the other window and aisle seats are taken—including, of course, 11A and 11C. The middle seats are the last to go.

It's illogical to think—sealed and strapped in a tiny fuselage screeching through the sky at a frightening speed—that an aisle on one side and an empty seat on the other would give a person a feeling of autonomy, but it does. The middle seat, shoulder to shoulder and elbows vying for armrests, is, in my opinion, the epitome of entrapment. I will do anything, even sit in the smoking section, to avoid a B seat.

But on this particular evening, I was on standby for a late trip from Dallas to San Francisco and had to take what I got. What I got was 11B. Oh boy, three hours in Claustrophobia.

As I boarded the already-crowded plane, I noticed 11C was standing by patiently at his seat. Obviously a frequent flyer, he knew he would eventually have to get up for two people, so he chose to stand and wait.

We made eye contact and he moved away to let me pack my carry-ons in the overhead bin and enter my assigned cubicle. "Welcome to Sardine Airlines," he said. *Well, at least he has a sense of humor,* I thought. We stood next to each other, waiting for 11A to show up, and carried on typical small talk.

Suddenly his eyes widened and I followed his studying gaze to a very attractive woman who was making her way up the aisle toward us. When she passed, he sighed, "How come they never end up next to me? Some guys get all the luck."

"Well, thanks a lot!" I replied.

Seconds later, however, she was back. "Excuse me. I think that's my seat," she said, nodding toward 11A, and 11C and I eagerly scrambled out to let her in. As we did, I stole a glance at him and found his eyebrows in a raised position. "Some guys get all the luck," he repeated in a whisper, indicating that stock in 11B had suddenly shot up in value.

I had a premonition: This was going to be *some* trip.

There are subtle ways that people have of indicating, early on in a flight, whether or not they are interested in engaging their fellow passengers in conversation. Burying one's head in a book or a briefcase is a signal easily read by all but the most indiscreet of travelers. Usually you can tell in the first minute or so what to expect, and the woman next to me let us know right away that she was up for conversation.

I say "us" because from the start I had 11C hanging over my right shoulder making sure I never had one private moment with the brunette in 11A. I considered giving 11C my seat, but he would never have gone for such an obvious tactic. Besides, that would have put me on the outside; and I knew if I was in 11C, I would dip into the conversation cordially, and then excuse myself to my ubiquitous yellow legal pad.

I don't usually seek out this kind of animated dialogue unless I'm the center of attention. It comes from all those years on stage, I guess. This was definitely outside my comfort zone. I wanted to fly with this experience even though I was scared. Being in 11B was going to force me to relate as a human being—something that as a "Christian singer, author, and songwriter" I can avoid doing if I so choose. In the "Christian World" I can get away with thinking I'm something more than human; but on this plane to San Francisco, I was just the guy in 11B. This was one time when "Fasten Your Seat Belt" had other implications. For the next three hours, I leaned my seat back, and 11A and C leaned into a lively exchange that had my head rotating like a lawn sprinkler. Three hours trapped in 11B between two bright and captivating people. I kept my seat belt fastened the whole flight.

Those three hours went a long way toward changing my concept of what Christians commonly call "witnessing." Believe me, when you're strapped into a 600-mile-an hour conversation in 11B at 30,000 feet, all those neat books and seminars on "How to Share Your Faith" go flying out the airplane window. If I could re-write those seminars and books, I would try something like, "How to Be Normal," or "How to Enjoy People," or "How to Be a Part of What's Happening Around You."

Half an hour into the flight and halfway into finding out what each of us did for a living, the flight attendant came by with beverages.

"I'd like a beer," said 11C, leaning for his wallet.

"White wine, please," said 11A, reaching for her purse.

"I'm buying," said 11B, pushing back both the wallet and the purse. *I can't believe I'm doing this,* I thought. *Is this anything like the wine at the wedding, Jesus? Something tells me you won't find this part in the witnessing book.*

We had already found out that 11A represented an interior design firm that specialized in decorating corporate offices. Now we discovered that 11C represented a furniture company that specialized in furnishing corporate offices, which immediately set off a mad exchange of business cards, brochures, and ideas. My neck felt as if someone had turned up the water pressure on the sprinkler.

"And what do you do?" they asked inevitably.

I knew it was coming, but there was no way I could have been prepared.

"Uh . . . music. I write and perform my own music. I have a couple of books published as well."

No, I didn't tell them I wrote Christian music or Christian books. It was difficult, but I found ways around it. I wasn't ready to tell them I was a Christian. Not when they were just starting to like me, and not when I was finding out I could actually carry on normal conversations with normal people.

We followed my lead into discussing music, writing, and the arts, then on to a brief dip into politics, and finally the subject of religion came up. Halfway through the flight, my moment came. 11C set me up perfectly.

"Would you believe the uncanny luck I have?" he said. "It seems as if almost every flight I'm on, I end up sitting next to some minister who wants to talk to me about God!"

"Well, brace yourself," I said, "'Cause it happened again!"

(Rule #1 in John Fischer's book on how to witness: Be a knowledgeable person. Have something to talk about. Don't just read Christian books and Christian magazines. It's a big world out there, and the Lord is the Lord of it all. If Jesus is the way, the truth, and the life, you should be able to start anywhere and end up with Him. Paul did this in Athens. He started with an idol to an unknown god and ended up with the resurrected Christ.

Rule #2: Don't tell them you're a Christian too soon; they might just happen to like you. And then when you finally do tell them you're a Christian, they might decide to like you anyway, which means that because of you, they will have to reexamine their whole idea of Christianity in the first place.

In this case, they had to like me because we were all having too much fun.)

"No! You're a minister and you bought the drinks?"

"Ever hear of the first miracle of Jesus?" I asked.

"Wasn't that when He changed the water to wine at a wedding?" asked 11A.

"Yes. How'd you know that?"

"I used to be a Baptist." And we were off.

For the next hour and a half we talked about miracles, Christians, TV evangelists, Catholicism, Baptists, faith, family, relationships, living together, life, death, Jesus Christ, and 11A's boyfriend who was waiting for her in San Francisco—the one she couldn't decide about because she left one in Dallas, too. (We understood how this could happen.)

By the time we landed at San Francisco airport, there wasn't one thing that I wanted to say about the gospel of Jesus Christ that I hadn't said. Yet none of it was forced, planned, rehearsed, or manipulated. And none of what I said was received as a sermon.

I'll never forget saying goodbye and walking away from baggage claim realizing that I had just been the best witness I could be by simply fastening my seat belt in 11B and going along for the ride. For in the energy, excitement, and sensuality that was flying around row 11, there was also a Holy Spirit very alive and well in the middle of it all.

SO WHAT WAS THE QUESTION?

——— 24 ———

If a generation that started with questions and ended up with Jesus tried to start the next generation off with Jesus, wouldn't that generation eventually have to go back to asking questions—the very ones it already has the answer to? Can you find Jesus without looking for Him? Can you have the answers without going through the questions? Is it possible to circumvent this natural process of seeking and finding?

Is it possible to have all this dropped in your lap? Can you receive, find, and enter without asking, seeking, and knocking? Well, I suppose you can, but wouldn't it be rather rude and presumptive not to knock first? If a person has come by all this so easily, who's to say it wouldn't be just as easily taken away? After all, "Easy come, easy go."

In seeking there is a glory that must be guarded. The parables of the lost sheep, the lost coin, and the lost son show a persistent Father bent on finding. Amazingly, God plays this game by the same rules as we do. If He is that persistent about finding us, how can we expect to get to Him any more cheaply?

We have seen this played out repeatedly on the stage and screen: lovers in slow motion running, gliding, sailing, swimming, floating toward each other's embrace. Why do we never tire of these scenes? Because they are a picture of God and man seeking each other, reaching out from something missing inside and holding tightly to it once it is found—each calling the other its own.

The important issue here is ownership. The answer doesn't become mine until I own the question, even if it means the dark horror or the empty loneliness of it. I might know the answer intellectually, I might be able to write books about it; but until it touches the aching questions of my heart, the answer isn't mine.

In the movie *Back to the Future*, the mad scientist is braced against the clock tower in a heavy storm. In one hand he has an electrical cord that goes to a lightning rod on top of the tower; in the other, a cord that will link up to the flux capacitor in his DeLorean time machine and send it and Michael J. Fox back to 1985 from whence they came.

I like to think of that cord as going deep into the hardest questions of my heart, and the other, to the answer from God. Until I connect these—and the question must be mine, a known and felt extension of my need—answers are no more than an empty cord dangling from the clock tower in the rain. The lightning will come, but it will do me no good.

We have a problem with having all the answers without owning the questions. Like the math homework we did in grammar school by writing in the answers from the back of the book, we get a 100 percent on our homework; but we never own anything from the experience that will give us any kind of score on the final test.

"But wait a minute!" you say. "Once you've found Christ, isn't the search over? Aren't the questions answered? Isn't the longing satisfied? What about all those great hymns about hope realized, like 'My Faith Has Found a Resting Place?' Well, hasn't it?"

Let me ask you: Are all your questions answered? Is your longing satisfied every moment of every day? Is the search over? Do you know everything there is to know about God? That scene where God and man embrace, does it happen only once in a lifetime, or does it happen over, and over, and over again? Do you sing "It Is Well With My Soul" only once, or do you sing it repeatedly against the backdrop of each new trying situation you face?

U2, the Irish rock group enjoying so much success in this last half of the eighties, had a controversial song that became a hit—at least controversial to those who know and care that three of the four members of this group are Christians. The song is entitled "I Still Haven't Found What I'm Looking For." When the song was released, immediately a minor uproar arose among their Christian following. Does this mean these guys aren't really Christians? Are they saying Jesus isn't enough? Are they leaving Christianity for something else?

But what they say is purposeful. These are careful artists; Bono, the lyricist of the group, takes great pains with his words. So it is no accident that their clearest gospel statement to date comes right up against this yearning lamentation. Maybe he's trying to tell us something:

> You broke the bonds
> You loosed the chains
> You carried the cross
> And my shame
> And my shame.
> You know I believe it
> But I still haven't found
> What I'm looking for.[1]

Two different recordings of this song were necessary to bring out its full meaning. The first, on the "Joshua Tree" recording, is somber and plaintive in tone, fully capturing the album's pictorial image, the gnarled silhouette of a Joshua tree standing alone against a desert sky.

The second, on their soundtrack recording, "Rattle and Hum," is entirely different. It is performed with a simplified rhythm and a black chorus. The style is entirely gospel and the tone is exalting, jubilant, electrifying.

I walk away from the first wondering. I walk away from the second with my eyes sparkling like a child's on Christmas morning. In this setting, "I still haven't found what I'm looking for" takes on a new attitude, as if the whole song reverberates with the question, "You mean there's more?"

Yes. Always.

Those who are satisfied with what they have, have what they have. Those who keep asking, seeking, and knocking will find more.

THE LONGING HEART

25

O the glory of the longing heart
O the aching of the wind
The groping fingers straining in the dark
To know what lies beyond the end.
Eternity is trapped in time
Beauty tarnished by the beast
Hope expires at the finish line
Where the universe is creased.
State the answer; don the uniform
Throw conclusions at the soul
Cash the question; kill the unicorn
Press neatly at the fold.
But still it opens at the budding rose
Still it wonders at the child
Still it knows what it refused to know
Who makes wild horses wild?

O the glory of the longing heart
Casting questions to the wind
Let it carry the soul searching far
Let it bring it back again.
But not so far that it will lose its way
Not so near that it will scorn
Near enough to give itself away
Far enough to know it's torn.
So give the longing heart room to roam
Let the truthful seeker speak
For in the seeking it will find its home
And in the finding it will seek.
O the glory of the longing heart
O the aching of the wind.

—John Fischer

I slept but my heart was awake.
Listen! My lover is knocking.

—Song of Songs

PART III

ASK SEEK KNOCK

$\mathcal{A}$ conversation I had with myself:

"Excuse me, but where does that door go?"

"No one knows."

"Have you tried to find out?"

"Yes, but it's locked. You can see for yourself."

"So you just stay here in this room?"

"Yes, we like it here; we have everything we need. It's very comfortable, and nobody really wants to go any farther."

"How long have you been here?"

"It depends on when you got here. Some have been here most of their lives."

"What do you do with your time?"

"Oh, we're quite busy. We have meetings to attend, officers to elect, committees to serve on, evaluations to give. Not to mention seminars and classes and games and social events and—"

"Has anyone thought of knocking?"

"And—what?"

"Has anyone thought of knocking?"

"On what?"

"On the door, of course. Has anyone tried knocking on it?"

"Oh no, we would never do that; we have too much to do here, and besides, you never know what might be on the other side. There have been a few who have knocked and the door has opened for them, but they never came back. We figure if He wants us to move on, He'll come get us."

"Wait a minute. Didn't He tell us to knock and the door would be opened?"

"Yes, but we already did that. That's what got us in here in the first place."

"How do you know He meant for this to happen only once?"

"Well, you know, Revelation 2:20 and all."

"But how do you know that's the same door? In the same breath He told us to ask and seek, too. Is that supposed to happen only once?"

"That's what I always thought. You *ask* Him into your heart and you *seek* until you find it. I found it. You know, I'm going to have to ask you to excuse me. I have an important meeting to begin."

"Fine, but first, can you please ask those people over there who are blocking the door to move?"

"Suit yourself. Are you going to see if it's locked?"

"No, I'm going to go knock on it real hard."

"Well, don't say I didn't warn you. You never know what might be on the other side."

"I know. That's why I want to find out. Besides, if He opens the door, what have I to fear?"

KNOCKING ON FAMILIAR DOORS

——26——

For four months now I've been back in the habit of jogging three or four days a week. Once, I had developed a regular pattern of running, but an injury, the nature of which I have since forgotten, had broken the string of succession I had built up. Running definitely is a pattern—far easier to maintain once begun than to begin once put aside.

I am more determined now than ever not to lose what I have regained in this endeavor, the tangible benefits being more evident as I grow older. The periodic lower back pain I used to experience, especially after so many hotel beds, is gone. Recovery time from the aches and pains of abnormal exertion (i.e., clearing brush in the yard or shoveling snow in the driveway) has been significantly reduced. And the extra fat around my waist signaling the onslaught of the back half of my years has been checked and driven back to a tolerable level.

But beyond all these benefits, the discipline of running has been inextricably tied to other more important areas of my life that have needed attention for some time.

Discipline has not been a virtue I could truthfully claim. I have even disguised my lack of discipline as a kind of superior spirituality enabling a more flexible freedom in the Spirit. "Go with the flow," "Be available," and the always handy "Whatever" have been catch phrases from the freestyle sixties, behind which I have crouched too many times in my own laziness.

At long last, I am beginning to weave the loose threads of an extended adolescence into a mantle of adulthood more appropriate to my age and the gray strands of hair stealing in over my ears. For many men in my generation, growing up—sacrifice, hard work, doing what one must do—has been a difficult thing to come to. Running seems like an invisible nylon line giving strength to this resolution.

It is a delicate weave. To remove this new-found discipline would endanger the whole network of thread.

I've lost track of the interplay—the cause and effect. Has running made me more disciplined, or does discipline make me run? I no longer know; I simply do not want to do anything to upset the weave.

They play on each other in the warp and woof of this new mantle. Running is to me now a symbol of new ground gained with each step. It reminds me of what I truly want but easily forget. Each time out, the sluggishness of compromise is forced out through the pores of my skin, and the oxygenation of my blood sharpens my vision, clarifies my scope. To live a vital life, to go beyond barriers, to venture into new vistas of faith and experience, to throw myself with a certain level of passion into everything I do—a passion big enough to drive me beyond the point of pain where I am acquainted with setting up camp—this is why I run.

Sometimes I can even smell the smoke of imaginary fires urging me to stop and rest.

There's nothing terribly spiritual about this effort except that God deserves it—He's deserved it all along—and that's enough.

But lately I've made an important observation. Due to my schedule of concerts and seminars, I have had to take this habit on the road. No big deal—just an extra sweatshirt and pair of socks and, of course, those black running pants.

At first I thought it was merely coincidence, but now it's too predictable to deny. After four months of this, I can say without a doubt that it is easier to run when I'm away than it is to run at home.

I shouldn't be surprised by this; the reasons are obvious. New horizons, new surroundings meet me at every turn. It's becoming a way in which I acquaint myself with each new area. After flying so far, running is a feet-on-the-ground experience of exactly where on this blue planet the mighty silver bird has deposited me.

In just one month I have run through the wet streets of Spokane; on the artificial tarmac of a college in Virginia; through a wealthy, oil-rich suburb of Tyler, Texas; up and down hills in the shadows of Yosemite Valley; along perfect sidewalks that crisscross Steinbeck's Salinas; and through the icy forbidden polar air of Saskatoon, Saskatchewan. Each new place offering new sights, sounds, smells, filling my senses with enough to distract me from any pain.

And I have an audience. I'm usually housed in a densely populated area, so I run amidst activity. People come and go, all obviously noticing and impressed with me, for even though some suited businessman may run 5 miles a day, as I pant by him on my 1.8-mile marathon, I'm the one who's running right now, and that's all that counts. I try to fight this, but I have to admit to feelings of superiority. I imagine these people as happy campers settled in around their cozy fires as I pass by, denying the warmth.

Finally, when I am on the road, I am focused—one place to be; one thing to do. No house to care for, no bills to pay, no wife, no children, no telephone, no mail, no messy desk. I can focus on this running like I focus on my traveling assignment. It can be either a release from, or a gearing down into, my singular reason for being there.

Not so at home. It's all too familiar. I pass the mailboxes, the barking dog, the farmhouse, the road to the dump, and I haven't even gone halfway. Each time I set out I think I'll be stronger, that this marked distance has got to get easier, but it never does. Sometimes it seems worse.

There's no glamor here as I pull on my black pants and a thousand things fill my mind—a thousand excuses to put this off until tomorrow. No new horizons, no new audience that hasn't already seen me before on this little neighborhood treadmill down to Hay Street and back.

But it's here that it means the most. It's here that I feel the pain. Sometimes it engulfs me even before I reach the barking dog. Everything feels heavy: my legs, my arms, my breath, my future, my marriage, my children, my papers pressing down on my desk. The pull can be so strong I fear I won't make it.

In these moments I learn the most, for these barriers are the strongest—the ones I meet every day, the ones that I have formerly stopped short of, the ones that challenge my faith and my commitment, that call me to throw myself forward with each step, challenging a well-worn path like knocking on familiar doors.

FROZEN SUNLIGHT

—————27—————

*B*right, clear, cold, windy—
such are the words for today. They show their stark side in my
mind as wind from the west slams hard against the back of the
house, rattling anything outside that's loose. Sometimes the gusts
are so strong that bits of snow and ice, impacted for days, are
torn from the roof and driven past the upstairs window where
I sit.

The small wood stove that we put up here in this room over
the garage will come in handy today. It hasn't seen much use
this winter—the electric baseboard heater works fine down to
about 20 degrees—but today, at 18 degrees, with the relentless
wind finding every conceivable crevice in my western defenses,
I need something with which I can fight back the cold.

In California, where I grew up, clear and bright were almost
always synonymous with fair and warm. It's taken me all of six
years here in New England to realize that clear and bright can
also mean bitter and cold.

There's a door ajar somewhere downstairs. It slams uncon-
sciously every few minutes. I don't like the feeling that some-

thing, however small, isn't fastened, hitched, braced, bolted, or tied down against the storm. I dash downstairs, check the porch and garage, and find nothing amiss. I return and hear it again. It's unsettling. I stoke the fire and gain security from its presence.

Life is deliberate here in New England. It shows all of its sides. In California the metaphors were simple: clear meant warm; cloudy meant cold. All the Sunday school songs worked. God speaks through the blue sky; His love pushes the clouds away; the rain may fall but there's a rainbow coming, blah, blah, blah. Right now there's not a cloud in the sky. The sun is sterling, it's colors, pristine; but step outside and a cold Arctic blast will rip the feeling out of your skin in minutes. This is frozen sunlight, and it's just as much from the hand of God as a California sunset. Today in New England, clear means cold.

An encounter with God is not always a pleasant experience. Sometimes the answers He gives us are not the ones we wanted. To turn to God, to have a clear, bright word from Him, may mean to face the harsh reality that's throwing itself against our defenses.

I turn toward the wood stove, and through a small window in front, I can see a steadily burning flame. Though my toes are a little cold, my backside is warm, radiantly warm. I remove my sweatshirt.

This stove generates a mysterious heat. It seems somehow to transfer itself to the surface of my body without heating the air. I can feel it on my face from a great distance, even deep into my skin, but I reach out with my hand and feel nothing. I notice objects in the room are warm to touch. It seems this warmth doesn't come from the stove itself as much as it comes from the things that hold it and give it back.

Something about the cold outside and this penetrating, radiant warmth inside feels right. Not that I never had this feeling in California (we've all known the security of being indoors on a rainy day), but in California it was more like a mood. We had fires there, even wood stoves, but they were nice, not necessary.

I want a life-and-death faith. I want my Christianity to be a matter of survival, not a matter of taste. I don't want a smiling Christian sun to come out and warm my day. I want to know the radiant presence of God in the midst of the harsh reality of frozen sunlight.

My wife does not share these sentiments. She would return to California in a moment—proof that this is not something inherent in the location, but merely something personal in my own pilgrimage. No doubt somewhere right now on a warm beach, watching the sun go down over the glimmering water, someone who grew up in New England is penning what great avenues of faith and discovery the westward ho has wrought. But for me and for now, the sun sets over an icy field, and like this day and like all of the days of my life, it means something.

JUST ASK THE METER MAID

————— 28 —————

$\mathcal{N}$ewburyport, Massachusetts is, I'm sure, not unlike any other eastern town whose parking facilities have not quite caught up to the growth of its business district. It's actually not as bad as some make it out to be. There are parking lots available that require, at the most, three blocks of walking to reach anywhere in downtown. For those coming from out of town for a few hours of shopping or eating, this is a small price to pay.

But for those of us who live in the area and utilize downtown shops for daily items, it takes a different sort of tactic. A card for your aunt's birthday, a box of envelopes at the office supply store, or a magazine at the smoke shop can turn into a major event.

For this kind of shopping, a standard street drama is being played out daily. Motorists cruise the narrow streets like linebackers looking for an opening in the parking lane. Experienced players learn to look for telltale signs of daylight—movement of a body in the driver's seat, white back-up lights flashing on, the approach of a driver to a parked car ten spaces up the street.

Then comes the well-placed block to allow the exiting car to open a hole while disallowing anyone else but you to fill it.

The final resort, when none of these plays prove successful, is to chance the loading zone, the fire zone, the handicap zone—or, if you're really desperate, the double park. But this is a serious gamble because, wouldn't you know it, the most dedicated police officer in the whole city is, of course, the meter maid. She walks the streets of Newburyport in rain, snow, sleet, or shine and affixes violation envelopes on the windshields of mal-parked vehicles.

We all know this woman. We park in fear of her. Some even hate this woman. She has the uncanny ability to materialize during the four and a half minutes you are standing in line at the post office getting a two-ounce letter weighed, and you left your car partially blocking the driveway with the motor running.

She is always dependable—the paragon of precision. Her uniform is pressed and her back is straight. Her hair is cropped short in a military cut, and her expression, unchanged. She has what seems to be a small tape recorder strapped to her waist with which she apparently keeps track of cars in the two-hour zone. She doesn't miss a trick.

All of our childhood fears of getting caught writing nasty things on the bathroom wall come to the surface when we see this woman. She is the dean we never wanted to confront, the teacher we were always glad we never had. She is omnipresent. She has eyes in the back of her head. And she has actually been known *to ticket her own car*! "By the book" is an understatement.

But another side of Newburyport lends a different view to this woman. It's a side hardly visible from the window of a Saab stalking the backfield.

This is the walking side; it belongs to those who live in town and hardly ever use a car. They pick up their groceries and sundries on Pleasant Street, have breakfast on State Street, and stroll the boardwalk every day just for the pleasure and the companionship. They know each other, these walkers—maybe not by name, but surely by face, and by smile, and by the predictable "Hello. How are you today?"

To these people, the meter maid is someone else entirely. She's an important part of the routine—one of the many smiles that make up a customary day. They have no fear of her, for they have nothing to which she can affix a violation. And she understands. She, like them, is confined to traversing this town the way it used to be done—on foot.

To these special people a great loss has come. A familiar sight among the walkers for almost ten years has been an elegant senior couple who have played a major role in this pedestrian drama. Always impeccably dressed in finely tailored clothes, they reflected their native Italy as if they had just walked off the set of *Moonstruck*. They both wore dark hats that contrasted their silvery white hair, and he walked with a cane—ever since he was taken out by an inside linebacker looking for a parking place in 1985. But the cane only made him appear more distinguished.

Exuding European grace and charm, they hardly belonged among casual tourists; they acted as if the whole town belonged to them. They moved through sparse days and the crowded days of special events with the same air, smiling at everyone, especially the children, and babbling on and on in Italian about something or other. They were a last remnant of the Old Country that few ever notice.

But the meter maid noticed.

That's why she attended his wake. She was the only one besides family and close friends who did. She came in full uniform and paid her respects without a word, but with tears flowing down her precise face.

If I wasn't in such a hurry to come to conclusions about someone's character, I might be in for more surprises like this. And if I wasn't in such a hurry to find a parking space and get my business done, perhaps I'd meet some people like this lovely couple before it's too late.

There's a whole different view of Newburyport—or any other town, for that matter—on foot. Just ask the meter maid.

THE CROSSING

29

*M*icah woke up to the heat of the early morning. It was the time of year when the night provides little respite to the heat of the day in the lower Jordan valley. There was hardly a stir in the camp as he arose from his blanket and made his way quietly to the river. The weight of the day hung heavy on his shoulders, waking him from an uneasy sleep and sending him off to a quiet spot to be alone. His legs took him there before his mind knew why.

It had been three days now since they made camp by the river. Three days and no word yet on the crossing. Just like Yahweh to bring them to the river's edge and let them sit for a while. Following Yahweh always kept them on edge, and though Micah should have known that by now, he still could not control his impatience. Why couldn't Joshua strike the water like Moses at the Red Sea? They already knew from the spies at Jericho that God had gone before them, protected them through the faith of a Canaanite harlot. That, too, was like Yahweh. Always the unexpected.

He stood at the swelling river and noticed that it had risen even more during the night. They would be crossing at the worst time—the harvest—when the river overflows all its banks.

But how? How would they do it? Some of the engineers among them had devised plans, even tested some, but they were all too dangerous with the river at this size. Joshua simply waited and said nothing. "Does he expect to hear from God?" some were saying. "Does he think he's going to be greater than Moses?"

The news of Rahab had stirred new faith in the camp, but not enough to overcome forty years of grumbling in the desert. Besides, none of Micah's generation had ever experienced the power of Yahweh firsthand. The miracles of God through Moses and Aaron had been passed down, but what is a story if you haven't experienced it? It's just a story.

He remembered his father. He had died in the wilderness along with the rest of those who would never see the promise. A twinge of excitement and wonder shot through his heart as he stared across the rushing water to the opposite side. There it was. The promise. The land flowing with milk and honey. The land that for all of them would be something they had never known in their lifetime. Home.

How proud his father would be of him! Micah wished his father could have lived long enough to see his son become a bearer of the ark. "Of all my priestly duties and responsibilities, there is none greater than to bear the ark of Yahweh's covenant with His people. It is the presence of God among us—the hope of this nation. Pray that you may be worthy, my son; pray that you may be worthy." Those words had been fingered in his mind until they glistened like the smooth stone he carried in his pocket. And now they had come true.

Micah closed his eyes on the river and prayed out loud, his words drowned in the water's murmurings: "Oh, God of Abraham, Isaac and Jacob, make me worthy to be your priest. Make me like Levi, Kohath, and my father, Elizaphan. Make me worthy to bear the precious signs of your presence and your covenant with your people, Israel. Make my arm strong and my heart large, and may the seed of doubt find no root in my soul."

Opening his eyes, he saw a figure coming to him down the gentle slope from camp. It was Caleb. He had the gait of an old man driven by the spirit of youth. He approached Micah and spoke excitedly in his raspy whisper of a voice, "I've just been with Joshua; he heard from the Lord. Last night. We will cross the river today on dry land and the ark will go first, before the people. Come, we are readying ourselves even now."

The two men returned to camp, Micah visibly scrambling to keep up with the old man's steady energy. All the way back he fingered his stone, thinking, *The ark first . . . on dry land . . . today? Make me worthy, Lord; make me worthy.*

They returned to find camp in a bustle; preparations to move had already begun. Officers were passing through the midst of the camp repeating instructions: "When you see the ark of the covenant of the Lord your God with the Levitical priests carrying it, then you shall set out from your place and go after it. However, there shall be between you and it a distance of about 2,000 cubits by measure. Do not come near it, that you may know the way by which you shall go, for you have not passed this way before."

You have not passed this way before. How those words danced in Micah's ears! Nothing again would ever be the same. Quickly he gathered his things and joined the priests at the holy tent, which was already being dismantled. Then he set to work with others of the household of Kohath, wrapping the lampstand and the sacred utensils of the sanctuary, stacking the tables and the altars. This was their sanctuary on the move. Micah wondered as he packed, *Will these sacred things ever have a permanent home? "You have not passed this way before."*

When all was prepared, Joshua came and addressed the priests. Micah listened intently. "Take up the ark of the covenant and cross over ahead of the people." Then looking directly in Micah's eyes he said, "When you come to the edge of the waters of the Jordan, you shall stand still in the Jordan."

Joshua then turned and announced that he wanted to address all the people, but Micah hardly heard. *Stand still in the Jordan?* What could that mean? Nothing about dry land? No striking of the water? What good would it do to stand in the Jordan with the ark? That's not going to get anybody across any river. He returned from these thoughts to hear the last of Joshua's speech to the people. ". . . when the soles of the feet of the priests who carry the ark of the Lord, the Lord of all the earth, shall rest in the waters of the Jordan, the waters of the Jordan

147

shall be cut off, and the waters which are flowing down from above shall stand in one heap."

So that's how . . . thought Micah as he prepared to hoist the ark up on his shoulder. *I'm going to live the stories of Moses!* Trembling with the weight of importance, Micah and the other priests lifted the sacred poles and set out for the river, each anticipating what it was going to be like to see water stand in a heap by the hand of Yahweh and the soles of their own feet. As they passed through the camp, men, women, children, even animals scampered to keep the prescribed distance, as if an invisible wall of power separated the ark from the people. Micah heard the words of his father once again as he realized he was in the center of the power, bearing it on his human shoulders. "Pray that you may be worthy, my son; pray that you may be worthy." And so he prayed in rhythm with his steps.

When they finally reached the riverbank, the priests rested the ark and prayed, gathering courage from one another's faith. Then with one more hoist of the ark onto their shoulders, they moved slowly, silently out into the water, with Micah in the front.

They took these steps gingerly. These were the steps of a miracle. Their feet were like the rod of Moses, and would open the way before them. Micah's heart was pounding with excitement and fear. He had never been this close to the hand of God. Step by step they moved ever so slowly into the water, feeling with each foot for a firm placement among the slippery stones along the water's edge.

When Micah was in over his ankles, he looked back; priests in the rear of the ark were still on dry land. Nothing unusual was happening, but then, they were not all in the water, either. But with each step the force of the water grew stronger, causing Micah to shift his weight to keep balance; and with each step, doubt began to swirl around his heart like the water around his legs. He repeated his prayer, ". . . and may the seed of doubt find no root in my soul." That seed was trying hard to grow. The water seemed to thicken with his every move, but the fear that gripped his mind was not fear of the water but the growing realization that they were farther in the water now and *nothing was happening.*

When he was in up to his knees, he stopped and looked back again. Those behind stood in ankle-deep water. Should they go

148

farther? It might be too deep to control. No one wanted to see the ark of the Lord of all the earth floating down the Jordan, the hopes of a nation with it. He repeated the words of Joshua: "When the soles of the feet of the priests touch the waters, the waters shall be cut off." Shall not the waters of the Jordan be cut off and stand in a heap? Did not Yahweh speak it? Where is He? Who is Joshua? Can we trust Him? These questions, some spoken, all thought, swirled in the water around the priests as they stood knee-deep in the Jordan River, desperately holding on to the presence of God.

Suddenly Micah spoke, the words coming from a place deep within himself where the truth was stronger than his thoughts. "Stand still in the Jordan!" As he spoke it, the memory of the eyes of Joshua gave him courage.

He looked back at the multitude of people swarming like ants down the hillside. He watched them back up on the bank and imagined how silly he must look to them. Had God brought them all this way to strand them and the ark of the covenant in the storm-swollen river?

Micah could hear the low sound of murmuring rising up off the shore, but it was quickly quelled by someone rippling through the crowd—someone who soon appeared in front of the multitude as they moved aside to let him through. It was Joshua. Cupping his hands he shouted to the priests with an authority that immediately embarrassed their doubts, "Stand still in the river! Wait for the power of God!"

They waited for what seemed like an eternity. Small stones carried along by the current nibbled against Micah's toes. It made him think of the stone he carried in his pocket. It was a sacred stone from an altar, cherished for years by his father. On the day he died, he gave it to Micah and said, "Here, my son. I want you to carry this stone for me into the promised land. I cannot go, but God has told me you will see it. Let this stone be a symbol of my faith that you carry on into the new land. Promise me. So be it."

"I promise," Micah had said. "So be it." These were his last words to his father.

"Micah, Micah!" One of the priests was shouting from behind him. "Micah, move forward; I'm no longer in the Jordan!"

Micah looked back to see the water lapping at the priest's

toes; and looking down at his own legs, he saw that the water had receded below his calves without his even noticing.

So the priests moved forward, following the water that was now rapidly diminishing. At last, amid the cheers of the multitude on shore, they stood with the ark in the deepest part of the riverbed. In either direction, they could see nothing but sticks and stones and mud.

And the people passed 2,000 cubits from the ark, a steady procession well into the afternoon—some praising God, some filled with laughter, some too awed to speak. Not until the end of that procession did Micah find out that the waters had indeed been stopped—but farther up the river, near the city of Adam. *So God has stood the waters up in a heap just as He said! He simply chose to do it fifteen miles upstream!*

As commanded by Joshua, the priests remained with the ark in the center of the riverbed until stones were gathered by one man from each of the twelve tribes—twenty-four stones to form two memorials. Twelve stones on the bank where they would set up their first camp in the promised land, and twelve stones in the riverbed at the feet of the priests—memorials to the faithfulness of Yahweh.

And as they completed their tasks, Micah took out the small smooth stone from his pocket and dropped it at his feet—the fulfillment of his promise and his own personal memorial in the bed of a river that went dry by the Lord's hand and the soles of his own feet. He no longer had to live the stories of Moses; this was his own story, his own history with Yahweh. *For you have not passed this way before.*

MEMORIES ON CD

30

*L*ately it seems as if everywhere I turn on my radio dial, I hear something like "Classic Hit Radio—Yesterday's Classics, Today's Class." It used to be that the classics were Bach, Beethoven, and Handel. Now they're Lou Christie, The Supremes, and Gary Puckett and the Union Gap. It's not only radio. *The Big Chill* sent first-run movies leafing through stacks of singles from the sixties and seventies for sound-track material, and even major television ads are tapping into the power of nostalgia—cashing in on yuppie memories.

Proof positive is the fact that my kids, ages seven and nine, know so many of these songs when we never play them around the house. These music memories permeate our culture. This is the age of the golden oldies.

There is definitely a lure to this kind of music, especially for my generation. I've periodically found myself tuned in to one of these stations in my car, coming out of a trance-like state when I reached my destination with no knowledge of how long I'd been under. For someone like me, whose tender years spanned the sixties, each of these songs comes packed with emotional luggage. In the course of three or four songs, I can fall in and out of love twice, relive the confusion of a major war, and feel the impact of John, Bobby, and Martin dying all over again.

Something about this isn't good. I've known it for a while, but I haven't been able to put my finger on it. There's something I like about this nostalgia—and I'm not sure that's good for me— and something I don't like. I finally realized what was wrong just the other day when "A Horse With No Name" was coming through my open window—background music for the house painters next door.

Like a deer frozen by headlights on a dark night, I was stunned by the past. I immediately thought of the old house on Waverly Street where I'd lived with three roommates in 1972. I remembered the freedom, the fun, the relatively few responsibilities. I remembered playing frisbee across the street on a warm summer night with the speakers turned out toward the windows. I even remembered learning to play this song, though I never knew what it meant: "I've been through the desert on a horse with no name; it felt good to be out of the rain. . . ."[1]

Suddenly I realized what was wrong. *I've already done this!* There's nothing classic about this music. A classic is something that has lived for years and will go on living regardless of what happens to popular culture. This stuff is simply a replay of the first part of my life! We're a generation anesthetized on our past. This isn't classic music; it's not even rock and roll—it's only memories on CD.

Rock and roll is rebellious, radical, and ridiculous. It shocks the status quo, asks the real questions of youth, and always looks funny compared to what is presently acceptable. Rock and roll wakes you up. It shakes something in your face. It isn't pleasant, and it's entirely present tense. It should never have been allowed a shelf life.

Don McLean was right about the day the music died. He gave it a decent burial, but we keep wanting to exhume it.

"No one who puts his hand to the plow and looks back is fit for service in the kingdom of God."

If there is anything right about rock and roll, it's that faith, too, is rebellious, radical, and ridiculous. It challenges the status

---

[1] © 1971 W.B. Music Corp. "A Horse With No Name." Used by permission.

quo, it asks the hard questions, and it always makes someone who's acting on it look a little funny compared to what is presently acceptable.

Faith is not a memory; it is a present-tense engagement with reality. It wakes you up, throws life in your face, and dares you to do something about it. Faith is unpleasant because it always asks you to do something you've never done before—if not, it is not faith. Faith can only live when I've been stretched into a realm where I must act on what I believe without seeing it. It takes no faith to dream about the past; that kind of dreaming slows down faith.

I want to live a life I haven't lived yet. I want adventure. I'm over here on the other side of the Jordan with battles and giants on every side, and someone keeps trying to seduce me with familiar songs of the Red Sea and life in the wilderness.

Well, I won't have it. We need to tie into a faith of our fathers, but not a faith of our own brief past. That's not faith; that's just a rerun.

I'm scanning the dial now. There must be at least one current rock station still alive. I want something new, upsetting, uncomfortable—something that suits life out here where the streets have no name.

The next time I hear a golden oldie and feel that tug of nostalgia, I'm going to think of the children of Israel wandering around in the wilderness listening to "Moses' Greatest Hits" and watching *The Crossing of the Red Sea* on video cassette.

I knew I'd heard that sound track somewhere before . . . "I've been through the desert on a horse with no name; it felt good to be out of the rain . . ."

I think I know what that means now!

ASK
SEEK
KNOCK

KNEE DEEP IN QUAYLE

—————— 31 ——————

I've had enough Quayle for one year. All during this election it seemed journalists and cartoonists had nothing but Quayle for breakfast, lunch, and dinner.

God sent the children of Israel manna in the wilderness; and when they complained and grumbled about the lack of meat, He sent a wind from the sea and dumped three feet of quail on their heads. It took them two days and a night to gather up the quail, and when they finally sat down to eat, God struck them with a plague "while the meat was still between their teeth." For the people who died there, they named the place *Kibroth Hattaarah*, The Graves of Greediness.

I understand this story because I, for one, have gathered up a good deal of Quayle meat from the media winds this year, but as soon as I get some between my teeth, I get sick. I shouldn't be surprised; I asked for this.

It finally dawned on me that, like it or not, Mr. Quayle is a pretty fair representation of me, at least in the areas that we find it easy to take issue with him.

I suppose if I had fought in and survived Vietnam, or had followed my conscientious objection and served in a civilian capacity, or had even run away to Canada, I might be able to enjoy Quayle for dinner. But in my generation—and the Vice President's—these boys were the minority. Most of us figured some way out of the draft.

I don't know if these stories about Quayle using family influence to avoid combat duty in Nam are true. But I can truthfully say that if, at twenty years of age in 1967, with my youth and the best years of my life ahead of me, I had known someone who could have pulled strings to keep me out of a war no one understood then (and few do now), I would have told him to pull. Judging from the attitudes of most of my friends at the time, I wasn't alone.

The fact is, I avoided the draft through a ministerial deferment and then never went to seminary. Check the seminary records of those years, and I'm sure you will find them proliferate with dropouts a few years later. Either God issued a tremendous call to the ministry in 1968, or there were a whole bunch of guys like me with the same idea. This particular piece of Quayle meat turns sour right away in *my* mouth.

Many critics charge Quayle with being shallow, uninformed, unintelligent—a pretty boy with a head full of air, whose major accomplishment in life is a low golf score. This portion of Quayle proves quite tasty until, again, I take a good hard look at myself.

One of my mentors during the early seventies used to call me "Golden Boy." He was purposefully trying to get me to not trust in the natural abilities, good upbringing, and fortunate opportunities life had so far provided me. A good deal of what I have gained in life has come easily. If I look at Dan Quayle and wonder if he has earned the right to take on the vice presidency of the United States, I have to look at myself and ask the same question about my life and its responsibilities. I can't chew on Quayle, accusing him of being uninformed, and then be unwilling to do what is necessary to inform myself. Actually this man is a lot closer to me than I really want to admit.

A lot of the uproar that has come against Quayle from my generation has come from this generation's inability to deal with its own sins. Jesus said, "In the same way you judge others, you will be judged, and with the measure you use, it will be measured to you." He doesn't even have to do anything to bring on this reciprocal judgment; we bring it upon ourselves—it's human nature. We always criticize in someone else what has somehow managed to escape a similar scrutiny in us. The Quayle meat we're all getting sick on is our own sin, and it carries with it an awful plague.

I've decided I'm going to take a positive approach to this man in the White House. If I run across some journalist or commentator having Quayle for lunch, I'm not going to join in. Instead, I'm going to assume they're pointing something out about me, a fault I need to hear about and take note of. Whatever I find objectionable about this man is something I most likely have to come to terms with in myself. In fact, it's impossible for us to find fault in others that doesn't have its seed in us. To be innocent is to be without judgment. So when I'm tempted to get a tender morsel of Quayle between my teeth, I'm going to remember that there's a disease carried by this kind of indulgence—a disease that takes us straight to the Graves of Greediness.

THE BYPASS

32

I love to read newspapers. It started when I lived in the San Francisco bay area and got hooked on Herb Caen's column in the *Chronicle*. One of the hardest things about moving east was not being able to call the *Chronicle* "my paper" anymore. But time smoothes out these little adjustments, and I am now fully entrenched in the daily ritual of the *Boston Globe* with my morning bowl of Nutri-Grain.

By the time my wife heads upstairs for the shower, I am well into Mike Barnicle's column, a much more caustic, confronting one than Herb Caen's. His favorite themes are people inexorably caught in bureaucratic red tape, a consumer being clearly ripped off by an evasive manufacturer, or the senseless killing of an inner-city youth as told through the eyewitness account of an elderly woman who is watching her once peaceful neighborhood come crashing in on her while there's nothing that she, the police, or the city seem to be able to do about it. It can often be a sharp splash in the face on an early morning.

I frequently pick up *USA Today* when I'm away from home. This upbeat daily tabloid features a full color satellite view of the world; and from up there, everything usually looks pretty good. It always has a resilient, positive attitude. In reporting a plane crash, the *Globe* would mark the number killed; *USA Today* would headline the survivors. Robert Schuller probably quotes *USA Today*.

But just because I hit myself in the face every morning with Mike Barnicle doesn't mean I'm any closer to the world he writes about. As much as I would not like to admit it, I may have *Globe* literary tastes, but in actual living experience, I'm much closer to the safer satellite world of *USA Today*.

But is it really safe? Is my little New England town nestled into the coast thirty-five miles north of Boston, like any quiet suburban neighborhood, any more safe than the city it's trying to escape? What sort of hidden horrors lurk behind these neatly manicured lawns and brightly painted clapboard walls? There is much here to escape the scan of a satellite view.

I'm sure we could keep a suburban Mike Barnicle quite busy out here writing about the uncle who "takes care" of his niece— in more ways than one; the wife who hides the bruises; the husband who hides the bottle; the widow who keeps the pills going long after the pain is gone; the teenage pregnancy no one will ever know about.

Or how about turning Mr. Barnicle loose in our own churches to do some in-depth, behind-the-scenes, eyewitness accounting of our families and friends? My own family history, which to most people appears to be the perfect evangelical Christian model, would be a pretty cold splash in the face on anyone's morning if the whole truth were told. I don't think I'm unusual, either.

The issue is not how far suburbia is from the city; the issue is how far removed we all are from reality—how much we tell and don't tell, how much we face and don't face.

I'm not trying to focus on the negative just to be pessimistic. I simply know from my own experience that hope means little outside of a real encounter with despair, forgiveness means little apart from facing sin head on, joy means little without real tears of sorrow, and comfort isn't worth anything without real pain.

We all have these experiences; we just prefer not to read about them the next morning. We have our own ways of diffusing reality so we don't have to feel it hitting us square in the face. We like the full-color satellite sweep.

I recently spent three days at a small midwestern college. Late the first night I needed some medicine for a cold. So I went to the only place I could find open and picked my way through the beat-up cars and scattered shopping carts to find a place to park. Mud-filled potholes, trash, and gravel obscured most of the fading parking lanes; but no one seemed to pay any attention to them, anyway. Inside, I stepped over the partially swept floor and unshelved merchandise to find the medicine I was after. Glancing over a primarily low-income black clientele, I imagined I probably had more money in my wallet than most of them see in a month. I tried to cover up my nervousness by being overly casual. At the check-out stand, I picked up *USA Today.*

The next time I needed something, I found a neat, well-stocked little market located halfway out of town on a street everyone referred to as the bypass.

FUMIGATE

33

$\mathcal{I}$ know it can get much worse than this, but it's hard to imagine. We have three pets: two cats and a dog. They are all kept indoors, and they all have diarrhea. Apparently I've switched their food one too many times. We ran out of cat food, so I gave the cats dog food; then we ran out of dog food, so I gave the dog cat food. According to the vet, my smorgasbord diet has been too much for their little stomachs. I won't upset yours by taking you through all the messy details, but I must admit, I've thought more than once about drowning them all.

Marti (who hates to be referred to as "my wife") came up with a better idea. We leave on vacation in a week. She wants to get out of the house, lock up all the windows and doors and bomb the place with a disinfectant. She wants something that will wipe out all residual smell—something that will reach back into the most remote places a cat could go and magically make all traces of their mistakes disappear.

She wants to fumigate.

It occurred to me that if Marti could, she would deal with

the world in much the same way. She would fumigate it. Spray the whole place with something that would disinfect it of sin and evil—something that would penetrate deep into all the dark corners, even down into the cracks in the wood floor where the stuff has soaked in, where you can still smell its traces but you can't get it out.

Before you think I'm trying to discount this simplistic approach, I must tell you, I admire this quality. Marti genuinely loves all people whether or not they know God. A direct quality of God that she exemplifies is spoken of by Peter in 2 Pet. 3:9, "He [God] is patient with you, not wanting anyone to perish, but everyone to come to repentance."

I can say without equivocation that this is a good description of what is in Marti's heart. She doesn't want anyone to perish. If she could touch a button and fumigate the hearts and minds of everyone in this world so that we could all live together and love each other, she'd do it.

I, on the other hand, come from a different school. I happen to think there are a whole bunch of people out there who deserve to go to hell. My idea of fumigation wouldn't just remove all traces of sin and evil from the world; it would take out large groups of people as well. They're a despicable, evil lot, a surly sample of humanity. We'd all be better off without them.

I'm not sure where this thinking has come from, but I know it isn't right. If God is not willing for any to perish, then how come I am? This is a truly humbling verse for me, because I've gone through most of my life perfectly willing to see any number of people perish. As long as I get in, what do I care? As long as I'm on the inside, what do I care what happens out there? It's a sad commentary, but from this perspective, the only motivation for evangelism is to assure me of my own salvation or improve my spirituality in some way. There's no real human compassion in it at all.

The Old Testament does express a kind of vindictiveness. In the Psalms, David lays a lot of evil wishes upon his enemies in vindication of himself. But David didn't see the whole picture. He saw only shadows. He didn't understand the cross. The cross has changed everything about the way we should view the world.

In the cross, God was reaching out to the world in love. "God so loved the world that he gave. . . ." In the cross, God said, "I'm providing a way I can love you. It's sin I hate; it's you I love. I am not willing for any of you to perish, so I'm paying your debt. The only way you'll face my judgment is because you want it that way. That's not the way I want it. I want us to meet here at the cross, where my blood, not your own, covers you."

We must view the world with the heart of God. Marti is a lot closer to that heart than I am, though I'm learning. Some will say her theology could weaken into universalism, but mine weakens into fascism, and I'm afraid the Christian community in America is much closer to my danger than hers.

If we stay close to the cross, we will be neither fascist nor universalist, but compassionate people who love the world as Christ loves it—reaching out in reconciliation, caring, and forgiving, hating the sin, loving the sinner. We will see every person as one for whom Christ died, and that in itself gives them tremendous worth. We will look at the world and not be willing for any to perish. And if we stay close to the cross, we will realize that the only way we can ever think there are people who deserve to go to hell is when we find our name on the list of the most deserving.

Meanwhile, I've got sick pets to deal with. Believe me, I'm counting the days until vacation.

FUMIGATE: CONCLUSION

34

$\int$o we went on vacation and left the cats out on the screened-in porch with instructions to the neighbor for feeding and for changing the litter box. We returned a week later to find our porch turned into a bomb site. Every place *but* the box had been hit.

When I picked up the dog at the kennels, which doubles as a veterinary hospital, I asked the vet about my problem. She told me that unfortunately there wasn't a whole lot I could do. One of my cats (or both) was definitely upset about something. It was a behavioral problem. "He knows where the box is; he's obviously trying to tell you he's unhappy about his environment or the way he's being treated. If you really love these animals and want to keep them, about the only option you have is to take them to an animal behavioralist."

Now, I believe God gave animals for the benefit of man. He told Adam to name them and subdue the earth. And I believe there is a place for pets in our lives, especially in a family. The friendly wag of a dog's tail, the cat curled up on the corner of the couch, the children having living things to cuddle, play with, and learn to care for—all these serve an important function in any family. Animals even reflect human personality in some ways and can teach us certain things about ourselves. But there are times when having an animal goes beyond the limits of service or companionship. This was one of those times.

Take my cats to a shrink? Not on your life! How does this happen anyway? Do my cats lie on a couch and purr out their problems? Does the cat psychiatrist speak to them in soft, soothing tones? Does he want to see us together or separately at first? This was definitely too much. I knew how to solve the problem.

When I got home I went straight for the cats and spoke sternly. "Listen here, fuzzballs, you need to know that I could drown both of you at the drop of a hat and have no conscience about it at all!"

The cats looked up at me as if to say, "Oh yeah, Domehead? You don't have the nerve, and we can use your bed for a litter box any time we want!"

Now I know why those books on a hundred ways to kill a cat are so popular.

I went into the next room to cool off, and then I started thinking. Animals *do* seem to reflect human personality. Everyone's seen the old man walking an ancient dog whose face looks just like his master's. If animals act the way we treat them, then for me to be hostile toward these cats is to have them be hostile toward me in some way, and refusing to use the litter box would certainly be a good start.

Our treatment of people is probably not much different. Hostile treatment usually gets a hostile response; and love, even though it may not be immediately returned, at least provides an environment where it can grow.

One who parents with the attitude "God told me to subdue you, kid, so you better straighten up . . . I drown cats!" is most likely going to have a rebellious child on his hands. Although there are exceptions, a loving child is usually one who has been loved, and an angry child is one who has not.

Two of our friends have three teenagers who are like love factories. Because we live a few hours apart, our families get together for whole weekends, and those times are always drenched in hugs, kisses, and affirmations. Personally, I'll take as much of this as I can get. To believe my worth as a matter of faith is one thing; to have a teenager hug me and tell me how handsome I am is another.

Where did they get this ability? Most teenagers I know don't make a habit of affirming middle-aged balding men, even if they are family friends. It certainly wasn't their stable upbringing. During early childhood, their parents were deeply immersed in the drug culture of the seventies. These children endured divorce, multiple moves, various financial catastrophes, and adjusting to a new father. But through all of this, they've been consistently and unconditionally loved by their mother. They've always been treated with respect. They've been encouraged to think, to question, to come up with their own solutions—even to make their own mistakes. Their house has always been a haven for them, and for other teenagers in the neighborhood, a place where they can be themselves. How many seventeen-year-old sons wake up at midnight so they can have a couple of hours alone with Mom?

In contrast are the foster children this family often takes in. (Mom has a weakness for stray cats.) Their bristly hostility reveals immediately the different environment they've been raised in. Even then, it's amazing to watch a loving, accepting atmosphere begin to break open the hardest shell.

Why are heavy metal bands so successful? Why do kids enjoy being assaulted by this hostile, violent music? Why do they get a kick out of banging on each other's heads for a few hours? Could it be someone's been banging on their heads at home for 16 years? Do they, like my cats, respond to hostility with hostility?

I'd like to say that I cleaned up the cats' mess, put the box back where it belonged, and loved the cats out of their behavioral problem. It would provide a nice tight conclusion to the points I've been trying to make. But alas, that's not quite the way it has worked out. I did all these things, and the problem lessened, but it didn't go away. We can't tie everything up with a neat bow; life isn't like that. Love doesn't always *work*, and it doesn't always make things work out the way we want. Love is patient; love is kind. If we love these cats, we're simply going to have to put up with their messes.

Come to think of it, I don't always put all my stuff in the right places all the time. I'm glad someone loves me enough to want to keep me around anyway.

169

THE HOLY AND THE COMMON
——————— 35 ———————

$\mathcal{T}$here is a fundamental difference between righteousness B.C. and righteousness A.D. *Fundamental.* The clue to this difference can be found in the relationship—on either side of zero B.C.—between the holy and the common.

For B.C. righteousness, the holy and the common had to be kept separate, like oil and water. Out of twelve tribes of Israel, God ordained one of them to devote their entire lives to the holy and the uncommon. They were the Levites, and their mission was holiness—handling holy utensils in the temple, carrying out sacred routines, offering sacrifices for the people, changing their clothes a lot, and staying away from parties.

Which, of course, left everyone else the common tasks of digging in the ground, pulling heavy carts, lugging water pots around on their heads, bearing children, and fighting wars. (Once in a while, though, they did get to throw a party.)

But that's the way it was then, and that's the way it was supposed to be. Separate it; calculate it. Make a clean break. Spell it out to the people. Holy over here, common over there. You guys are to be holy so you can represent what holiness is to all these other common guys. They will have to keep coming to you to be cleansed.

For a classic slice of B.C. righteousness, consider this selection out of Ezekiel 44:

> "But the priests, who are Levites and descendants of Zadok and who faithfully carried out the duties of my sanctuary when the Israelites went astray from me, are to come near to minister before me; they are to stand before me to offer sacrifices of fat and blood," declares the Sovereign Lord. "They alone are to enter my sanctuary; they alone are to come near my table to minister before me and perform my service.
>
> "When they enter the gates of the inner court, they are to wear linen clothes; they must not wear any woolen garment while ministering at the gates of the inner court or inside the temple. They are to wear linen turbans on their heads and linen undergarments around their waists. They must not wear anything that makes them perspire. [*No sweat.*] When they go out into the outer court where the people are, they are to take off the clothes they have been ministering in and are to leave them in the sacred rooms, and put on other clothes, so that they do not consecrate the people by means of their garments. [*Wouldn't you love to be around one of those guys!*]
>
> "They must not shave their heads or let their hair grow long, but they are to keep the hair of their heads trimmed. No priest is to drink wine when he enters the inner court. They must not marry widows or divorced women; they may marry only virgins of Israelite descent or widows of priests. They are to teach my people the difference between the holy and the common and show them how to distinguish between the unclean and the clean."

That's just a sampling of B.C. righteousness. The Bible gives chapters of minuscule detail where these delineations are carefully separated out. But fortunately for us, Jesus came and changed everything.

He drank wine, let His hair grow long, and was frequently seen at parties. As far as we know, He didn't change His clothes, and He perspired like any other man. Once, when He was praying, He perspired so much that blood was actually forced out of the pores of His skin. Jesus must have smelled like a common man.

Not only that, He appeared to profane even what the self-appointed Levites of His day regarded as sacred—desecrating their holy customs through Sabbath healings and fast food in the grain fields on a holy day.

In Jesus, there is much to be found that is common and much to be found that is holy. This is what is so different about righteousness A.D. We find the holy and the common occupying the same place, for in Jesus Christ they meet.

Even His conception is a meeting of the two as the Holy Spirit joins with the human race in that common sanctuary of the womb.

Mary birthed Him like any other woman: in pain, in sweat, through shrieks of fear and suspirations of relief; and He came forth like any other baby: blotchy, wet and red, screaming a protest to the harsh reality of His new environment.

My own wife's reflection on birth is most certainly common to Mary's:

> I think the body senses when somewhere
>> along the way,
> Something important comes out of nothing.
> It is the time dreams are born—
>> before the water breaks
> And all the tears spill out.
> Your birth is a special thing among births.
> Something about it quiets me and gives cause
>> for wonder
> As I warm my hands on its brightness.
> The corridor was a rushing wind tunnel:
>> in the center brilliant lights
>> gathering dark significance
> And sparks of swirling conflict.
> Time stood still and faces froze
> As tense down to my skin
> Your cries reached heaven and then fell.

There is a cemetery in my soul
Containing yet-to-be born dreams
    where,
Hearts broken, spill tears
When I discovered I was not alone.
The universe shook apart
    by the invitation
    of a star
No less brighter than you.
In the deepest of reality,
Love talked—
    and He spoke through you.
                    —Ruth Martin Fischer

The holy *and* the common: this is the wonder and the adventure of Jesus. For once the common has been touched by Him, it ceases to be common. Jesus not only brought us salvation, He brought holiness to our common life.

He touched the bread and the wine, and our meals are never the same. He occupied the womb, and birth is sacred. He wept, and our tears no longer go unnoticed. He breathed this air, and suddenly there is meaning and value to human life. And He bled red blood, giving this body, in all of its functions, a sacred mandate, once known, and still possessed by the Son of God.

And still, with all this hope and promise and all that is to be redeemed, B.C. righteousness lives on. Separate it; calculate it. Make a clean break. Spell it out to the people. Holy over here, common over there. You guys are to be holy so you can represent what holiness is to all these other common guys. They will have to keep coming to you to be cleansed . . .

HE COULD HAVE SAVED
THE WORLD

——36——

I don't know what happened to
that Phil Keaggy," Ted Nugent said after Keaggy left Glass Harp
to join a Christian community. "He could have saved the world
with his guitar"[1]

I read that quotation, and suddenly the hopes and dreams,
frustrations and failures of twenty years of Christian music
flashed before my eyes. I saw the needs of a world still lost and
dying, untouched in so many ways by huge expenditures of effort, time, and money.

I was on a plane when I read the article, and I immediately
started to cry. It was such a poignant statement of lost potential—
of falling so far short of the goal.

"Oh, come on, John," you're saying. "One man with some
wood and a few strands of metal in his hands isn't going to save
the world." But one man with some wood and metal on His back
did save the world. And in every generation since, there have
been men and women who, knowing that, have done more with

[1]Contemporary Christian Music, January 1989.

whatever they had in their hands than any of us ever have. They may not have been able to save the world, but they certainly knew who did, and they risked everything to let the world know.

I once thought I could save the world with my guitar. That's why I started to cry. I once knew that feeling.

What happened? Well, I started out trying to save the world, and ended up trying to get a record contract. I started out trying to save the world, and ended up trying to find out what Christians wanted. I started out trying to save the world, and I'm still trying to justify myself to the First Baptist Church.

Somewhere along the line I compromised and took the easier, safer road. I listened, even though I knew better, to those who told me that if I was a Christian, my music was going to have to change. It was going to have to be Christian music, and even though no one knew what that was, I tried to find out. What I came up with was restrained, contained, stifled in some way. I was freer before when I could have saved the world with my guitar.

I listened to those who said my music must be sacrificed on an altar. It must take second place. And thinking I had only one heart to give, I gave half of it to the Lord and half of it to music, and both came out halfhearted. I knew better. When the Lord is in my heart, I can give all of it to everything I do.

I listened, even though I knew better, when they said that a Christian could never be popular with the world. I'd have to sacrifice too much and compromise too much to get there. So I settled back into second best where it was safe, where I didn't have to deal with my ego, while I pampered it and gave glory to God.

Then, when I was that far in, I didn't have to listen anymore, because I came up with this one myself: I didn't have to be the best. No one would ever say it; I just knew it. As soon as I realized I was playing only for Christians, I no longer had to compete with the Knopflers, the Claptons, and the Dylans. In fact, when I played my best licks, I got criticized for not ministering. It seemed pointless to extend myself, and so, even though I knew better, I gave up being the best.

I could have changed the world with my guitar. But wait! Why am I talking as if this were some kind of epitaph? It's not, or at least it doesn't have to be. I still have the rest of my life, and so do you, and so does Phil. Is there anyone out there fool enough to think he can still change the world with his guitar? I don't think anything's going to happen until there is.

U2, at a crossroads early in their history, decided to play for the world instead of for Christians. They had to make this choice against the counsel of their church. A Christian record company consultant told me of a joke he once pulled on a major Christian label. He slipped in an early tape of U2's "I Will Follow" as a demo among new artists for review. When the record company executives laughed at it, he informed them that they had just rejected what would probably be the world's most popular arena rock band. They went on laughing, and U2 went on to tell the world whom they follow.

Just the other day, I was on the phone with my travel agent, who doesn't travel in Christian circles. He surprised me by saying, "Hey, I know someone who I think you know, or at least is in your line of work."

"Oh, really? Who?"

"Phil Keaggy."

"You're right," I said. "I know Phil; I've even played a few concerts with him. Incredible guitar player, isn't he?"

"Oh yeah, the best! I followed him like a hawk in the early seventies, and then he just dropped out of sight. Just lately I heard he was in Christian music, so I figured you'd at least heard of him."

Got into Christian music and dropped out of sight. I thought, *That about says it all.* Perhaps it's happened to a lot of people as far as the world is concerned. People become Christians, and they drop out of sight. They become Christians, and they settle into the comfortable environment of Christian friends and Christian experience. But the room is getting too small. It's time to start knocking on the door again.

"Phil's recorded quite a few albums since then," I said. "I'll have to get some for you. Funny you should mention it. I just finished reading an article about him in a magazine I write for. I'll get you a copy of that, too."

"That would be great!" he said excitedly. "Too bad we never heard any more of him. I always thought he was one of the best."

"He is," I said, and hung up the phone.

IS IT WORTH IT?

37

*W*rite about this," my wife said, looking at me through bloodshot eyes at 12:30 A.M., three and a half hours before I had to get up to meet a 6 A.M. flight for a five-day trip. "Write about what we're feeling right now."

Write about that? I thought four hours later as I drove to the airport on a stomach as empty as the freeway in the predawn darkness. *Write about the fact that it's not working—her working and me on the road? Write about the feeling of our family flying apart? Write about the fact that the sitters aren't lining up as I planned for the kids after school? Shall I write that I'll be calling from St. Louis after I speak in chapel to see if the elderly lady can sit tomorrow afternoon? It's a half day for grade school children, while the junior high sitters are in school all day; if she's not available, I don't have any other plan.*

Shall I write about the emotional trauma my wife feels these days when I go on the road? Since she went back to work, I've been playing the role of Mr. Mom, Father Knows Best, and Garp all rolled into one. I'm not sure I should do that. Then again, a good dose of reality is what people have come to expect from me. But this feels like a double dose. This isn't just knocking;

this is throwing myself up against the door.

I sit in 6D, climb over long shadows and clear skies above a western Massachusetts morning and decide what to do. O.K., I'll do as my wife said; I'll write about it. I'll disclose how, after pouring twenty years into a career that I can't explain to the man on the street—a career without insurance, a pension plan, or retirement—that I look in the mirror sometimes and wonder if it's worth it. I'll explain that I wonder how I'm still doing what I'm doing now, much less what I'll be doing twenty years from now. That after twenty years, ten albums, and three books, I'm back to square one, trying to scrape up enough money to go into a studio with a band to record live demos of my new songs.

Yes, I'll even say I'm scared. That at my age and with my responsibility, I should know a lot more than I do about what I'm doing and where I'm going. And if I really feel brave, I'll describe how I feel this almost all the time.

But I should also write about last night—about the song I wrote for the annual dinner of the Essex North Chamber of Commerce where Marti is the president. No great spiritual coup here, just a good old human song about responsibility to the community—about realizing that you can't take from a community without putting back into it, or you will leave nothing for the next generation. Somebody left something for us; we have an obligation to do the same: "Somebody passed it down; somebody pass it around."

I'll point out that by the end of the evening, *everyone* was quoting it. Even the featured speaker, M. L. Carr, "the spirit of the Boston Celtics," quoted from my song, rewriting his whole speech based on excerpts from it. I'll write how people came up to me afterward with testimonials about what the song had meant to them—one reporting tears, another clutching a copy of the lyrics to her as if it were her child.

It will be encouraging to remember how one song—even one line from a song—can say more than a thousand sermons. It can quicken the mind and stir the heart; it can talk to the spirit in a person before that person even knows He's there.

And I will recount some of the times people have come up and told me a song led them to Christ or kept them from suicide. Yes, I'll write about all of this and then step back and let someone else wonder if it's worth it.

I feel like asking the same question to the guy in front of me in 5D. The flight attendants have just found out he is a new father and are making a big scene. In fact, it appears that his wife is in the hospital right now and the baby has just been born. *And he's in a business suit on a flight to St. Louis?*

I feel like asking *him* the question: "Excuse me, sir . . . ah . . . this thing that you do . . . tell me . . . is it worth it?"

HEAVEN'S DOOR

38

Knock, knock, knocking on heaven's door.[1]

—Bob Dylan

*D*arn. I was all set to go, too. Edgar Whisenant said the Rapture would happen by sunset last night, and here I am filling up an airline seat with my full body weight on the way back to Boston. I was looking forward to not having to pay my mortgage this month.

But wait—what's this? A small headline in the *Charlotte Observer* catches my eye: AUTHOR POSTPONES RAPTURE 'TIL TODAY. Sure enough, Edgar has revised his schedule. The Rapture is now going to occur at 10:55 A.M. Eastern Daylight Time, today. A quick check of my watch reads 10:17 A.M.

From the airline map, I calculate that in 38 minutes we'll be

---

somewhere over the vicinity of Washington, D.C. What's it going to be like to be at 37,000 feet during the Rapture? Will I go quicker?

10:23 A.M. E.D.T. The meal comes. Should I bother? From the looks of it, I don't relish the idea of making this my last.

10:28 A.M. E.D.T. I start to think about what it will be like if this thing is really going to happen in 27 minutes. There's a momentary lightness in my heart as the cares and worries attached to normal life on earth fly away at the thought. This could be it: the final door! But then I am rebuked by another thought. Should the most exciting thing about the Rapture be getting out of this world, or getting into the next? Is the greatest thing about heaven simply getting rid of my cares on earth, or is it the joy of finally being united with Christ, the object of my longing? "For me to live is Christ, and to die is gain." The fact that it took me a few minutes to come up with that longing part concerns me.

What about all the earthly cares I'm so eager to escape? I'm supposed to be casting those cares somewhere. Have I let the cares weigh me down so that the supposed escape from them would overshadow the anticipation of seeing my Savior face to face?

10:31 A.M. E.D.T. I suddenly am aware of the man next to me. Does he know? This is kind of silly. Edgar Whisenant has got to be some kind of religious nut. Jesus even said no one will know the hour or the day of His return. Kind of rules out 10:55 A.M. E.D.T., doesn't it?

Still, you can't help but wonder. There's got to be some substance to his argument. This guy has a whole book of research on times, dates, prophecy, and numbers. God's movement in history does seem to fit into numbers—40 years, 40 days, 7 years, 3 days. It does seem remotely possible that someone could add up all these prophecies and come up with an accurate time. What if the Lord really said no one more would know the hour or day of His return except Edgar Whisenant, and Jesus said that last part to himself, under His breath? I mean really, why bother trying to explain Edgar Whisenant to the disciples?

"You live in Boston?" I ask the man next to me. Better be sure. I would hate to leave this plane at 37,000 feet and never forget what I could have said in those last 15 minutes. How do

I approach this? "Excuse me, but have you heard about that guy who said the Rapture is going to happen in a few minutes, 14 ½ to be exact? Well, he's probably some quack, but just in case, are you ready to meet Jesus Christ?" Sorry, I just couldn't bring myself to it.

Luckily he helps me by asking what I am writing about, so I relate Edgar's prediction. We both laugh, and I find out the man's a Christian. He's been teaching a Bible study for twenty years. He even shares with me some ideas out of the book of Romans that he has just learned.

Phew! I'm off the hook on that one. But what about the rest of the people on the plane? When should I start singing "I Wish We'd All Been Ready"?

His wife comments that she hopes this meal isn't our last. "I would hate to go out on this one."

10:43 A.M. E.D.T. Forget about the rest of the passengers; what about the rest of the world? What about my friends who don't know Christ? How can I be so glib about this? I hope the lack of concern I feel is not a lack of true compassion but an indication that I really don't believe this thing is going to happen. Yet even when I try to imagine it's true, just to see how I feel, I'm coldly unconcerned.

Once again, I remember the passage in 2 Peter: God is not slow about His promise to return. He's simply waiting to give more people a chance to respond to His grace. He doesn't want anyone to perish. *How much of that attitude is in my heart?* I wonder.

10:54 A.M. E.D.T. Well, this is it. I wonder if I should unfasten my seat belt.

10:55 A.M. E.D.T. Nothing.

10:56 A.M. E.D.T. Nothing.

10:57 A.M. E.D.T. I strain from my aisle seat to look out the window, wondering if this could be something like being in the air during an earthquake. Suddenly I remember one of those tacky religious paintings I once saw of the Rapture. Planes were crashing into skyscrapers, traffic was snarled as cars with absentee drivers when out of control, and everywhere wispy souls whooshed up through the air. Either we have a pagan pilot and for some reason I've been left behind, or Edgar missed a few calculations. I gaze out the window a little longer. No wispy souls. 11:24 A.M. E.D.T. Touchdown, Logan Airport, Boston. Well, Edgar, it's back to the drawing board. And me—well, it's back to the world a little wiser. Thanks anyway, Edgar.

WORLD CLASS

39

$\mathcal{O}$nce the fastest runner was the one who could beat everyone around the block. Winning was a simple, tangible thing: You simply outran everyone else. I once ran a foot race to gain the hand of a popular girl in school . . . quite gallant for the second grade.

But in this present society of sweatband endorsements, the winners are world class. TV, magazines, and athletic stores full of personalized pumping paraphernalia have focused the attention on a few. We all know who the best are; their names and images are emblazoned on our minds and our sports equipment. They're not the best on the block; they're the best in the world.

Total dedication and total concentration are the requirements in this race; after all, the world is a big block. It seems there is always someone who, for the one who has exhausted all physical, psychological, and emotional limits, can finish a second faster, jump a centimeter higher, throw an inch farther. Records are made to be broken.

Roger Craig, running back for the San Francisco 49ers, explained it this way in his preparation for the 1988 NFC Championship game against the Chicago Bears: "I know it's going to be punishing out there, so I condition my mind for it by pushing my body to the limit so I won't have to second-guess myself when I'm on the field. I do everything I can to get my mental capacity as strong as I can."

For Craig, "everything" includes running hilly courses of 5 and 8 miles near his home three times a week. The other three days he sprints, running 100's and 220's with 30-second rests in between, running until either his mind or his body gives out. In addition to these workouts, he goes to two chiropractors and one massage therapist to keep his physical apparatus tuned to its optimal performance level. "You have to treat your body like your automobile. If it breaks down, you rebuild it."

The rest of us settle into the couch on a winter Sunday afternoon and watch him slice his way through the defensive back field and wonder how he does it.

Even when the opposing team finally brings him down, you can see his mind falling forward. They might get him on the 3, but his eyes are in the end zone. He just never stops running.

I think of Roger Craig while I'm jogging 1.8 miles in 22-degree weather. It will take me 20 minutes to complete the neighborhood course down to Hay Street and back—hardly world class, but it's something for me.

Somewhere between the couch and Roger Craig in the Super Bowl, you'll find me, trying to stay in some kind of shape.

On one hand I'm tempted to think well of myself as one who has found a reasonable symmetry in life; after all, there are excesses on both sides of this equation. I'm sure Roger Craig has trampled over important values on his way to winning; and there's no doubt about the deficiencies of the couch potato. I can feel pretty smug as I turn around on Hay Street for the .9 miles back to my house. I've given up something, but I'm not overdoing it.

Suddenly I catch myself slowing down: my pace is comfortable. 1.8 miles a day. I can do this; I've worked up to this plateau. My breath doesn't heave anymore and my heart's built up strength. It's comfortable at a 1.8-mile jog. It's comfortable, but I'm not. I'm bored.

My pace quickens as I suddenly have a vision of Roger Craig leaping like a gazelle through a hole in the front line; of knees churning high like the blades of a harvester cutting through winter wheat. His eyes fix solidly on some distant goal while his body rotates around them; when pushed or pulled off course, he somehow reestablishes himself, twisting, turning, another angle on the same destination; he is determined to go farther than anyone's ever gone and give more than anyone's ever given.

More world class visions come to mind as my heart pounds harder to keep up with this inner mental accelerator, the kind of pictures that bring tears to my eyes even while watching sports specials on airline flights without the earphones. A hurdler is timed perfectly between strain and step; a pole vaulter goes face to face with the sky, curling his back like a dolphin. A runner readies himself to explode from the starting block; a chest thrusts forward to break the plane of tape; arms are held high in victory—the culmination of hours and hours of sacrifice and hard work, overcoming obstacles millions of viewers will never know or appreciate.

My feet pound harder, faster on the pavement as the words of Paul come to mind: "I do not consider myself yet to have taken hold of it. But one thing I do: Forgetting what is behind and straining toward what is ahead, I press on toward the goal to win the prize for which God has called me heavenward in Christ Jesus."

In my mind's eye, as my house comes into view, I see my own personal obstacles, those things which still lie between me and that high calling. I see defensive backs dodging and darting to throw me off balance, to bring me down. But even if they get me on the 3, I know my eyes are in the end zone.

And as I turn into my driveway and begin the cool-down of a walking pace, I realize that I will never stop running—never stop living like this. Roger Craig and Paul and I have something in common. There's more at stake here than a neighborhood jog: This is life, and I am a world-class liver of it.

THE WIZARD OF UZ

—— 40 ——

I spoke once, but I have no answer—twice, but I will say
no more.

—Job

*I*n the land of Uz there lived a man whose name was Job.
What did this man learn from his life—from the pain and suffering, the wise and unwise counsel, from all the unanswered
questions—288 of them to be exact, including 78 questions from
God?

Even after his health and wealth were restored, he never
knew that God and Satan were bartering over his soul in heavenly places. He never knew that his story was going to be chron-
icled in the most important book in history and read for thou-
sands of years by millions of people, that it would be pored over
and picked apart by generations of scholars, that it would con-

tinue to be debated in the classrooms and literary halls of history, that indeed whole volumes of books about him would stand in seminary libraries, and songs and plays would be written and performed about his life.

All he knew was that things were going pretty good for a while, and then suddenly everything got really bad, and then it got good again. Did he ever get his questions answered? No, but he did see God, and apparently that was enough. "My ears have heard of you but now my eyes have seen you," declared Job after facing God's 78 questions. "Therefore I despise myself and repent in dust and ashes" (Job 42:5–6).

What did Job do to repent of? "I spoke of things I did not understand, things too wonderful for me to know" (Job 42:3).

He spoke too soon.

He tried to answer questions he had no business answering.

He tried to explain his life.

He tried to put tab A of his theology into slot B of his experience, and it didn't fit.

He tried to make sense of his life instead of learning to live it, regardless of what was happening to him.

I think a similar repentance is in order today. Christian culture in America too often speaks too soon. We have rushed to fill the void where only wonder should be—wonder, and doubt, and suffering, and ambiguity, and worship. We have knelt too freely at the cultural shrines of easy answers rather than live a courageous asking, seeking, knocking life—open, honest, and needy before the Lord and before the world.

True believers—who, like Job, have learned their lesson—ask why. But they are wise enough, and childlike enough, not to always expect to understand the answer.